SEEDS FOR CHURCH GROWTH

Published by
Norman F. Somes
P.O. Box 43,
Jacksonville, OR, 97530.

Available from Amazon.com, createspace.com and other retailers

More Review Comments on Seeds for Church Growth

"It's good work... helpful and engaging... so many good ideas for ministry in one place... has a style that makes it an enjoyable read."
The Rt. Rev. Michael J. Hanley, Bishop of Oregon.

"I can easily imagine church leaders and committee members being able to discuss, inwardly digest, and use the abundant suggestions. It is very clear....tone is so hopeful and optimistic.... taken the scary stuff out of evangelism and brought it down to a practical and imminently do-able level. I thoroughly enjoyed it and believe there is a real need for it.
The Rev. Anne K. Bartlett, Retired Rector,
Trinity Episcopal Church, Ashland, Oregon.

"One thing I really like... it is a practical guide supported by the research, not one full of theories but lacking nuts and bolts."
Dr. Thomas E. Glover, book author and parishioner.

"I got many good ideas from reading it... thoroughly enjoyed it..."
The Rev. Court Williams, Rector, Saint Thomas Episcopal Church,
Eugene, Oregon.

"It provides pithy, easily accessible suggestions.... demands little investment in reading before it bears practical fruit. The author's style is clear, lively, friendly, and compassionate. On behalf of parish clergy everywhere, thank you for the gift of time, experience, Spirit, and maturity that is this project."
The Rev. L.D. Wood-Hull, Rector, Saint Barnabas'
Episcopal Church, Portland, Oregon.

SEEDS FOR CHURCH GROWTH

A Practical Handbook for Episcopal Rectors

Norman F. Somes

"For all who proclaim the Gospel
and all who seek the Truth."

CONTENTS

ACKNOWLEDGMENTS

My thanks to the succession of wardens and vestries and to the people of Saint Barnabas' Episcopal Church in Arroyo Grande, California who gallantly gave of themselves that we might receive the stranger. Together we took steps set out in this handbook and with joy increased our congregation 150 percent. In this case, the harvest laborers were many, far too numerous to mention them all here. Yet among these sterling characters, several made outstanding contributions: Neita Oates, (Director of Children, Youth, and Family Ministry), Ron Williams, (Minister of Music), the Rev. Richard DeBruyn, (Deacon), and Grace Ramsay, (Parish Secretary). Throughout, I was blessed with the participation and endless support of my wife, Patricia.

Greatly valued was the collegiality of the Central Coast clergy; I drew much from their support and inspiration.

The Rt. Rev. Richard L. Shimpfky, former Bishop of El Camino Real, was a keen observer of our church-growing efforts and source of much encouragement.

Of many mentor figures in my development, two stand out. I acknowledge with gratitude the example and guidance of both the Rt. Rev. William E. Swing, former Bishop of California, who ordained me and who kindly reviewed this book, and the Rt. Rev. James L. Jelinek, former Bishop of Minnesota, under whom I gained field training for two years as seminarian when he was Rector of Saint Aidan's, San Francisco.

Pastoral ministry is foundational to growing a church and I extend my appreciation for grounding provided by the Rev. Dwight W. Edwards, former Rector of Saint Mary's, Pacific Grove, California, whom I was privileged to assist following seminary.

Much was gained from the contributions of others to this project. Firstly, I extend my thanks for reviews provided by Thomas and Carol Glover, the Rev. Randy Ouimette, Lutheran Pastor, Episcopal Bishops William E. Swing and Michael J. Hanley, and for the Episcopal Rector's perspective provided by the Revs. Anne K. Bartlett, Sara Fischer, Court Williams, and L.D. Woodhull.

Annie Offenbacher word-processed the several drafts with great understanding and patience.

Finally, I wish to acknowledge the cooperation and responsiveness of the CreateSpace design team.

FOREWORD

"At the least, Seeds for Church Growth would be of significance to a parish priest if one only made a running tally of what one's own approach to parish growth is and then compared it to the categories suggested in this book.

At its best, this book challenges one to see every aspect of ministry as having interrelated relevance to the whole and thus to church growth. At the core, Somes is convinced that the key motivator is seeking to assist new people in discovering a richer experience with God in a parish setting.

This book rings true to my experience in parish ministry and church growth. And it works."

The Rt. Rev. William E. Swing, 7th Bishop of the Episcopal Diocese of California, President and Founder, United Religions Initiative.

PREFACE

The Church is forever called to adapt, to be a flexible force for all settings and seasons. The Gospel will always need to be taken to the people in a manner most readily understood and received. Among the many who ministered to this reality were Saint Paul, Patrick, William Tyndale, Thomas Cranmer, John and Charles Wesley, George Whitefield, Jackson Kemper, Dorothy Day, and Billy Graham. But this book is not about the illustrious. Rather,, it offers guidance to those of today's Church in today's settings who wrestle the age-old question — how best to connect with those among whom we seek to share the Gospel?

Not all such endeavor demands deliberation, however. Consider the first evangelist I ever encountered. She appeared one day on the street of my childhood there in that distant suburb of London. I was playing with my friend Brian. We were nine years old. She was twenty I guess, with a pretty smile. She simply stopped and spoke with us. Of that conversation I recall just one thing but that one thing possibly shaped the rest of my life. She asked if we'd like to go to Sunday School with her on the coming Sunday; she was one of its teachers. No doubt my non-church-going parents were amused but they consented.

Come Sunday it was clear that our evangelist had been busy, for there were a half dozen of us, girls and boys excitedly chattering away as we accompanied her on that mile walk to church. There, week after week, I met Jesus. Well, I met pictures of him, stories and songs of him and I was taken with the one about him loving me.

Later in life, upon studying the Bible, I learned that Iris Marshall had daringly done what Philip did in Galilee upon encountering Nathanael and telling him of Jesus (John 1.45-46)* She had simply extended Philip's

---

* Biblical quotations are from the New Revised Standard Version unless noted otherwise.

invitation, "Come and see". That invitation has echoed down the centuries and is still ours, yours and mine, to make today.

Incidentally, the street on which I was born and raised is called Philip Avenue, but as a believer I was to encounter more "Godincidences" than this. As with gratitude I recall this formative episode in my life, I wonder just how many lives my evangelizing friend Iris Marshall opened to God's grace and to the knowledge of that divine love. Christ surely came among us seeking that we, congregation by congregation, individual by individual, take up our own unique Marshall Plan for the reconciliation of humanity to what God would have us be and do.

In 17th century England, Bishop Thomas Ken (1637-1711) penned this prayer which has since adorned many a church door including that of the parish I was privileged to serve.

O God, make the door of this house
wide enough to receive all who need
human love and fellowship, narrow
enough to shut out all envy pride and strife.
Make its threshold smooth enough to be no
stumbling block to children nor straying feet,
but rugged and strong enough to turn back
the tempter's power.
God make the door of this house the gateway
to thine eternal kingdom.

It is to this timeless prayer that this book is offered as extended AMEN.

June 11, 2012

Saint Barnabas the Apostle

And Jesus said to them, 'Follow me,
and I will make you fish for people.'
(Mark 1.17)

The hand of the Lord came upon me,
and he brought me out by the spirit of
the Lord and set me down in the middle
of a valley; it was full of bones... and
they were very dry... Then he said to me,
"Prophesy to these bones, and say to them,
O dry bones hear the word of the Lord
Thus says the Lord God to these bones:
I will cause breath to enter you, and you shall live..."
(Ezekiel 37. 1-5)

Chapter 1

ABOUT THIS BOOK

I undertook to write this handbook that it might assist the much-needed resurgence of our denomination. Certainly part of my thinking in its preparation were vicars of mission congregations. Confining terms to parish, rector, vestry etc. facilitated a less-duplicative text. Since most of the content might interest leaders of other denominations, a glossary is provided.

Most likely, the reader will recall the punch line of a joke made famous by President Reagan's frequent use of it.

With all this manure, there has to be a pony in there somewhere.

It serves to underscore the power of thinking positively: that things are not as bad as they seem, and that feats of derring-do will turn them around. Why start this handbook on such a note? Well, for forty years our denomination has wandered the wilderness of declining membership. The bones of our valley are often found to be very dry. Googling "decline in the Episcopal Church" reveals so much that explains causalities. Yet to rehash it here serves little purpose. Rather, let's think positively for despite it all, *there has to be a pony in there somewhere.* That is my belief and experience and a reason for this text.

You were moved to take it up and read it. Why? Do you seek to grow your church? Face it; while exhilarating, it's a challenging task. Respectfully therefore, I recommend you carefully assess the motivation and resources for such an undertaking, personal and otherwise.

*For which of you, intending to build a tower, does not
first sit down and estimate the cost, to see whether he
has enough to complete it?*
(Luke 14.28)

However, before delving into such things, I wish to clarify what is meant here by *grow*. Spiritual growth is the core of the issue at hand. To grow your church is to pursue Biblical injunctions of which the most profound is Matthew 28.19-20.

*Go therefore and make disciples of all peoples, baptiz-
ing them in the name of the Father and of the Son and
of the Holy Spirit, teaching them to obey everything I
have commanded you....*

Two millennia later, any church that truly wishes to grow must wrestle with, come to fully understand, and heed the reminder given to us by William Temple, Archbishop of Canterbury (1942-44).

*The church is the only society that exists for the benefit
of those who are not its members.*

Temple's stunning statement is surely unsettling for some within the church. Yet I believe that the growth of a church hinges upon its spiritual leader and at least the majority of a congregation coming to accept Temple's guidance and working accordingly. Growing your church means being Christ's disciple and laborer and, in particular, leading the congregation in the being-sent-out aspects of the Baptismal Covenant [1]:

*Will you proclaim by word and example the good news
of God in Christ?*

*Will you seek and serve Christ in all persons, loving
your neighbor as yourself?*

*Will you strive for justice and peace among all people
and respect the dignity of every human being?*

Now, let's return to the all-important *you* in this venture and employ a sailing metaphor. I say all-important because to you the rector, you the spiritual leader, the congregation will look in charting a course for the parish. The power of the Holy Spirit, working on the collective will of the congregation, will fill the sails, but it will be your role to decide the destination. Thus you will profoundly influence the efforts of the congregation to share with others the good news of God in Christ—in a word to evangelize. There, I've said it! Said the action word that too many Episcopalians seem loath to utter and oft times cringe upon hearing. Instead, they prefer to talk in euphemisms, of welcoming, of inviting, as though the topic were tea and cake at 4 p.m. instead of a lifelong working relationship with Jesus Christ. So, explore how you feel about this word "evangelize", its use, its true meaning and all its implications. It's really a lifelong process, but make a start. This text will later point up avenues of useful exploration.

In reality, the word *you*, in this context, can have several meanings. It might include the vestry. It might also embrace the majority of the congregation. All of you might be enthusiastically committed to growth. Indeed, when you were being considered for Rector, it's quite possible that the Parish Profile clearly set down growth as a goal, that the Search Committee emphasized it in their recruitment probing, and that it was ultimately documented in the culminating Letter of Understanding and Offer of Employment.

Wow! You and they together were to grow the church. You have a clear mandate to do so. Brilliant! Outstanding! What an enviable situation, provided that it was not merely a public relations ploy and that all parties truly grasped the full implications of such a laudable goal — implications this handbook will address.

It will not shock you, I'm sure, if I point out that some parishes talk the talk but do not necessarily walk the walk. To be brutally frank, some parish profiles merely dress the window. *Didn't the archdeacon say that we should include that?*

Doesn't every parish seek to grow? Sadly the reality registers NO. We have those forty years of evidence to that fact. So, if you were called to a parish whose previously expressed desire to grow now seems to be hollow, don't give up hope. The parish profile may have been window dressing but you can still put it to good use as I will explain later. What really matters is, *do you want to grow your church?* That's paramount. It's akin to Jesus' question to his disciples.

> *But, who do you say that I am?*
> (Matthew 16:15)

Of course, it could be that your call to the parish involved no commitment to grow by any party, you included. It was to be a ministry of maintenance, status quo! Yet things have a habit of changing: local demographics, charismatic influences on the parish (Cursillo, Faith Alive, ALPHA, and Via Media) and, all importantly, you. The Holy Spirit labors away. The seed grows, albeit silently — your picking up this book for example. Perhaps it can still show the way to growth. I earnestly hope so!

The approach and structure of this handbook.

Are you a gardener? Perhaps not. You've been busy elsewhere I imagine. But as any gardener will tell you, a seed catalog can be a splendid thing. It can be very expanding and uplifting, stirring the little grey cells in exciting ways. Therein lies promise and, with care and perseverance, growth and fulfillment. It points up limitless things to try.

> *At the heart of gardening there is a belief*
> *in the miraculous.*
> (Mirabel Osler)

Not all things will flourish. Some are clearly unsuited to the setting, but there are so many alternatives that something is bound to be successful. The catalog remains a thing of endless hope. It's like that with evangelism and your church and this handbook. Its text sets out to offer seeds, myriad means, small or large, fast or slow-growing, low-budget or costly, by which to bring growth to your congregation. For each seed a commentary and growing tip may be included as appropriate. It's all there for your perusal, selection, planting and nurturing.

> *A seed hidden in the heart of an apple*
> *is an orchard invisible.*
> (Welsh proverb)

Of course, Jesus talked about seeds. His community understood little about most things but they could grasp his messages better when he illustrated them with seeds. A seed might seem puny, yet its potential could be great. A seed might be silent in growing, yet its outcome could be glorious to behold. A seed might have promise, yet success hinged upon its nurture. It is no different with the seeds offered here.

> *I am about to do a new thing;*
> *Now it springs forth, do you not perceive it?*
> (Isaiah 43.19)

Some seeds will suit your parish soil and some will not. Some you may have planted already. Others will be new to you, so new in fact that they may, at first blush, seem threatening. Be assured that all have demonstrated growth and are well worth examination and use. Of course, some suggestions might appear to be conveying the obvious or even trite. For that the author apologizes yet simply wishes to be as all-embracing in this offering as his experience permits. While some suggestions may seem obvious, that may explain why they're so often overlooked.

What this handbook is not.

It is not a scholarly review and analysis of all that is published on the matter of growing a church. Rather, it is a compilation of proven actions, one that focuses upon the Episcopal ethos and you, one of its leaders.

It is not about your congregation's spirituality of giving, though many possible church-growing initiatives will necessitate more vigorous stewardship support with time, talent and treasure.

It is not about worship per se, though both existing members and newly attracted members will need the sustaining, enlightening power of a Spirit-filled Word and Sacrament.

Tend my sheep.
(John 21.16)

It is not about preaching quality, though the congregation will need to be educated, motivated and nurtured consistently if they are to *go therefore and make disciples of all peoples…* (Matt. 28.19a)

Feed my sheep.
(John 21.17)

It is not about pastoral sensitivity and care, though some congregation members may find growth disquieting and stressful. *Change is loss* my seminary Professor of Pastoral Theology* would frequently stress. The tuning of clergy antennae to the mood of the congregation takes on greater importance when change is underway.

Though this book is not about aspects just touched upon, growing a church underscores their parallel importance to the endeavor.

---

* Charles Wellington Taylor, Church Divinity School of the Pacific

Come labor on.
Who dares stand idle
on the harvest plain,
while all around us
waves the golden grain?
And to each servant
does the Master say
'Go work today.'
(Hymn 541, The Hymnal 1982 [5])

Chapter 2

THE HARVEST OF OUR CHURCH

When he saw the crowds, he had compassion for them
because they were harassed and helpless, like sheep
without a shepherd. Then he said to his disciples, 'The
harvest is plentiful, but the laborers are few, therefore
ask the Lord of the harvest to send out laborers
into his harvest'.
(Matthew 9.36-37)

What sort of harvest has the Episcopal Church been gathering in recent times? A comprehensive answer to this question is provided in the two following reports.

- Facts on Episcopal Church Growth. A new look at the dynamics of growth and decline in Episcopal parishes and missions based on the 2005 national survey of 4,100 congregations. C. Kirk Hadaway. [2]

- Episcopal Congregations Overview: Findings from the 2010 Survey of Episcopal Congregations. A congregational research report from Congregational and Diocesan Ministries, Domestic and Foreign Missionary Society, The Episcopal Church. 815 Second Avenue, New York, NY. 10017. By C. Kirk Hadaway, April, 2011. [3]

These two documents provide excellent coverage of the reported relationship between growth or decline and a host of characteristics descriptive of Episcopal (and probably other) congregations. As such, they are invaluable pointers for those who would understand better how to pursue the Great Commission.

Reference will be made to a number of Hadaway's findings as they pertain to the seeds for growth put forward in this handbook. One set of data will be dealt with here however. Hadaway [3] tabulates a comparison of the age structure of the USA with that of the Episcopal Church as drawn from a 2010 survey. He does this for five categories, children and youth, young adults (20-34), median adults (35-49), middle age (50-64) and seniors (65+). Using his data, the figures that follow show the relative proportions of each age group in the Episcopal Church expressed as percentage of the USA population in total.

Children and youth	54%
Young adults	50%
Median adults	86%
Middle age	144%
Seniors	231%

A clear picture emerges. In what might be viewed as understatement, Hadaway notes *Episcopalians tend to be older than the general population.*

While the Episcopal Church needs to vigorously pursue growth in general (addressed by Chapter 6), particular emphasis (Chapter 7) must be placed upon the two younger generations if the church is to be representative of society as a whole. Children and youth (that means of course young families) and young adults are under-represented to an extent that seriously jeopardizes the vitality and thus the very future existence of some Episcopal congregations.

To be, or not to be, that is the question:
whether 'tis nobler in the mind to suffer
the slings and arrows of outrageous fortune,
or to take arms against a sea of troubles
and by opposing end them.
(Hamlet's monologue, Act 3, Macbeth by William Shakespeare.)

Chapter 3

THAT YOU MIGHT BE SUSTAINED

It seems right to start with you and address your spiritual needs. As spiritual leader of a congregation turning its face toward growth, you will carry the heaviest responsibility and, sometimes, the greatest burden. It's important that you be sustained. This chapter is therefore about girding up, putting *on the whole armor of God* (Eph. 6.11), ensuring strength for whatever lies ahead.

Jesus said, *Take my yoke upon you* to be sure, but also added *and learn from me.* (Matthew 11.29) It is with such learning, his example, in mind, that I propose the first five seeds. So, let's break ground noting that:

> *The best time to plant a tree was 20 years ago.*
> *The next best time is now.*
> (Chinese proverb)

Seed 1   **Spiritual Retreat Time**

If you haven't already done so, establish the practice of taking time out for a spiritual retreat and personal renewal.

> *Come away with me to a quiet place and get some rest.*
> (Mark 6.31b NIV)

Commentary

Ask around. Enquire of retreat facilities within, say, a driving distance of three hours. Retreat houses of monastic orders probably offer the best all-round setting for your needs. Plan to make the driving time part of your reflective experience.

> *By all means use sometimes to be alone. Salute thyself;*
> *see what thy soul doth wear.*
> (George Herbert)

Accept the injunction to *wear sandals and not put on two tunics* (Luke 6.9). In other words, go simply. Leave all your high-tech devices at home or at least in the car. Unwind. Disengage. In this time of prayer, listen with a hearing heart. Allow the Holy Spirit space to enter your being, your awareness of things around you in this new setting, and your encounters with strangers in your midst.

Growing Tip

In the recharging stimuli of the setting and the sharings of others, you may be pleasantly surprised to experience

- solutions surfacing to myriad problems that seemed insurmountable back in the parish

- ideas aiding initiatives for growth

- and perhaps even story lines for the upcoming sermon you were concerned about.

> *I can do all things through him who strengthens me.*
> (Philippians 4.13)

Seed 2 **Spiritual Direction**

Again, if you haven't already done so, carefully seek out and periodically meet with a spiritual director.

Commentary

Consider the demands of the tasks you are embarking upon. Growing a church must inevitably bring about change and, remember, change is loss. Change brings about confrontation from some parishioners as at the outset: *We've never done that before. Things are fine as they are.* And of course the classic: *Nursery! But I don't see any youngsters.* Later stages bring: *Remember the good old days? Now I don't know half of them.* Yes, striving to minister to the many inevitably invites grumbling from the few. You know the cause is right and that good things are happening and yet, at times, you assuredly will feel frustration and confusion and be troubled spiritually. You may also need prayerful guidance, retracing your footsteps back to the Gospel.

> *It's me, it's me O Lord, standing in the need of prayer.*
> (Gospel song, author unknown)

Growing Tip

Be very exploratory and deliberate in seeking out a spiritual director. Gather inputs from other clergy in the area, Episcopal and otherwise. Even upon reaching a mutually acceptable arrangement with your subsequent choice, stay open to the question, *Is this working out?* If it is not, don't hesitate to seek another spiritual director. Your well-being and ultimately that of your congregation is paramount. For readers not familiar with spiritual direction there is, fortunately, a considerable amount of published work available.

Seed 3　　　　　　　　**Collegial Support**

To further strengthen your means of personal support, increase your participation in meetings with local clergy.

Commentary

> *The teaching of the wise is a fountain of life...*
> (Proverbs 13.14a)

Your regular meetings with clergy peers can be an enriching time of mutual sharing, prayerful support, and encouragement. Within such groups there is much experience to be shared, knowledge of things tried, of efforts that succeeded and those that failed (and why), of pitfalls to be avoided, and of resources that can be called upon. In short, these gatherings can empower you.

Growing Tip

Since such meetings might serve as a sounding board for your church-growing thoughts, plan ahead and request agenda additions that might assist you.

Of course, the united efforts of local clergy can have great Gospel-sharing impact on the local community. As illustration, in Arroyo Grande where I served, Catholics, Episcopalians, Lutherans, Methodists, Presbyterians, and Seventh-Day Adventists came together each Good Friday to powerfully experience the message of Christ's Passion. Each Thanksgiving Eve, they similarly united to offer their multi-generational and multi-talented expression of Thanks to God.

Seed 4   **Diocesan Bishop's Support**

Once you are resolved to work to grow your congregation, share this decision with your bishop.

Commentary

Thereafter, plan to keep the bishop well informed of your evangelism endeavors. With each subsequent visitation to the parish, both in preaching and discussions with the leadership team, your bishop thereby has the ability to become an authoritative advocate for what you are attempting.

Also, keep in mind that the bishop receives a great flow of information, national and international. Some of this may pertain to and aid your efforts. Your actions have given the bishop the means of passing it on to the right recipient.

There's another reason why you do well to confide in your bishop. Some changes in the parish, thought essential for growth, might so annoy certain members that they fire off a letter of complaint to their *chief priest and pastor* — it's then that a bishop's understanding and support is invaluable.

As ordainer and overseer of clergy, and as chief priest and pastor visiting congregations, the diocesan bishop has standing and opportunity to be a persuasive promoter of church growth. Yet this powerful potential contrasts markedly with forty years of decline in our Church. Clearly not enough bishops have given evangelism sufficient priority. Nonetheless, each of you, keeping the bishop well informed on your church-growing efforts, may help fan the flame of evangelism that our Church badly needs.

Seed 5   **Evangelism Committee**

…, do the work of an evangelist; carry out
your ministry fully.
(2 Tim. 4.5b)

To give yourself essential leverage and team support, promote the concept of a parish evangelism committee.

Commentary

To the frequently used question in social gatherings, *And what do you do?* I once heard a cleric respond: *Oh me, I'm in sales and service.* I got a kick out of that. He was selling the good news of God in Christ and was serving his flock. Embarking upon church growth, you will, of necessity, do a lot of selling. It starts with explaining to wardens and vestry the need and functions for this key working group. You require their endorsement of its role over time in devising, adapting, implementing and overseeing numerous initiatives to bring about growth. Furthermore, you need to hear the vestry's aspirations, reservations, and guidance. Above all, they need to feel closely involved throughout this exciting venture. Participation feeds commitment.

At startup, be mindful of the need to get this activity into the hands and hearts of laity as soon as possible. Recruit and chair this committee only as long as it takes them to elect a lay chair person. Thereafter of course, stay actively involved.

In recruiting, start small. Initially recruit no more than six members to this committee. Open your meetings with prayer.

Growing Tip

Draw up a set of attributes that, ideally, would guide recruitment. It would be wonderful if candidates demonstrated:

- a scriptural understanding of evangelism

- a positive, accepting approach to newcomers

- consistency in attendance at worship

- a sacrificial level of financial support of the church

- the inclination to work as member of a team

- readiness to evaluate new ideas in a constructive manner

- the ability to think creatively

- willingness to follow through and get jobs done

In reality however, you will have to settle for less than the ideal person. God did so frequently and still got the job done using Moses, Abraham, Jacob and that cast of other characters all the way through history to you and me!

As the start-up committee envisions more and more initiatives, its membership will, over time, need to be enlarged and recast to achieve the emerging skill sets that tasks require.

The first five seeds are sown with the aim of sustaining you in this demanding but potentially very-fulfilling endeavor. They should provide you with support and the means of maintaining an attitude of optimism.

Optimism, that cheerful frame of mind that enables a
tea kettle to sing though it's in hot water up to its nose!
(Source unknown)

Your optimism for the tasks ahead assuredly will be raised by Chapter 4, Exploring Seed Catalogs.

READER'S GROWING NOTES

Chapter 4

....

EXPLORING SEED CATALOGS

....

(And sharing discoveries)

Seed 6 **Internet Revelations**

If you haven't done so already, now is the time for you to Google *church growth* and related topics. It is sheer revelation. Encourage evangelism committee members to do the same.

Commentary

At least in the committee's early days, use a portion of your regular meetings to have members share ideas that leapt off the screen. You might systematize the process by having distributed previously one-page blanks that call for input under headings such as:

- what is the activity?

- what adjustments might be needed for our congregational setting and ethos?

- roughly, what does it seem to call for in time, talent, and money?

Growing Tip

By their participation in this task, individual members will demonstrate their particular sphere of interest, a useful input to setting assignments later on.

Seed 7 **Evangelism Conferences**

Pay particular attention to one aspect of Googling "church growth" etc., namely publicity concerning upcoming multi-denominational conferences that address the many aspects of evangelism.

Commentary

> *When the Spirit of truth comes, he will*
> *guide you into all the truth; for he will*
> *not speak on his own, but will declare to*
> *you the things that are to come.*
> (John 16.13)

Sam Shoemaker (1893-1963), outstanding Episcopal preacher and celebrated author of over thirty books, would often say that if we want to experience the Holy Spirit we have to go where the Spirit may be found. Evangelism is a case in point. Ideally, from among clergy, wardens, vestry and evangelism committee, several should attend. In that way, they may experience and report more fully on the typically multi-layered program. Furthermore, subsequently, participants can spread the *word* more readily.

The atmosphere of such gatherings is highly charged with earnestness and enthusiasm, an infectious combination. The worship is uplifting. The workshops tell of so much activity that is tested and truly works. One comes away buoyed and feeling, *Yes, we could do that, and that, and…*

It should be noted that such conferences may also address educational and ministerial programs for existing members, an aspect important to any congregation but beyond the scope of this handbook.

Growing Tip

Those of you attending the evangelism conference have a great story to record and promptly share with the parish. Traditional mechanisms available are:

- a brief account (or series over several weeks) within the Sunday worship services
- a Sunday morning forum (or series)
- the parish newsletter
- the Sunday worship bulletin
- drawing attention to the availability of a document report

It is at this stage that you and your team are probably hankering to experience personally a growing church, one that has the flavor of your region. What do its facilities look like, feel like, and what do its clergy have to say concerning their endeavors? Seed 8 addresses this experience.

Seed 8   **Visiting Exemplar Congregations**

Use local clergy contacts established through Seed 3 to secure the names of congregations, say within three-hours driving time, that are growing demonstrably. Undertake a mid-week circuit of visits to several.

Commentary

There's little learned that we didn't learn from others. As to exemplar congregations, it hardly matters as to their denomination. Rather it's that your clergy colleagues feel such congregations have something to teach others in regard to attracting and motivating new members. This is yet further information to share with the committee and vestry. Once more, participation feeds commitment.

Most leaders of growing churches are only too pleased to respond positively to your request to visit. Going as a team of three is probably best in that you can divide up coverage. As a suggestion:

- for you, discussions with clergy and other staff about church programs in general

- for your team members: what might be learned about the facilities and their likely impact on the newcomer and

- what aspects of congregational life might be gleaned from the worship literature, tract racks, notice boards and the operations of the church administrative office

While your hosts can more readily respond to mid-week visits, the all-important Sunday worship has yet to be experienced. Engaging a supply priest at your parish can bring this about on one or more follow-up occasions.

Seed 9   **Sharing Findings from Visits**

Compile and distribute a report on the findings from your visits to growing churches.

Commentary

The initial recipients of this report would be wardens, vestry and evangelism committee members. However, it's not too early to inform others such as, for example, the chairs of Finance, Stewardship, Building and Grounds and Worship committees. Seed 7 (Growing Tip) suggested other dissemination possibilities.

Growing Tip

Having others read the report is clearly good, but not enough. The opportunity to question, to give feedback, to offer ideas and support is best accomplished in special parish meetings of which the Sunday forum is one option. Again, I say, participation feeds commitment.

Assuredly, by now, people are asking questions: *Are we equipped to do that here? What changes and improvements do we need to make The obstacles that we don't recognize? The things we tolerate that others might not? Just how inviting are we, really?*

Chapter 5 offers the means of addressing their very pertinent questions but, before going there, it's worth noting that every parish should learn from others, but that each congregation will have its own unique flavor and also its own unique initiatives.

READER'S GROWING NOTES

Chapter 5

GAUGING THE pH. OF THE PARISH SOIL

*Why do you see the speck in your neighbor's eye, but do
not notice the log in your own eye?*
(Matthew 7.3)

*Growth begins when we begin to accept
our own weaknesses.*
(Jean Vanier)

*Our remedies oft in ourselves do lie, which
we ascribe to heaven.*
(*All's well that ends well.* William Shakespeare.)

Seed 10   **Midrash on User Friendliness**

Take time in both meetings of the vestry and the evangelism committee
to introduce and explore the term *user friendliness.*

Commentary

Pose questions such as: *In what context have they heard it applied?
What does the term mean to them? Do they think it could be applied to
a parish? In what ways?* For the following meeting, ask them to come
prepared to gauge the user friendliness of the parish as experienced by
parishioners of all ages and, most critically, those people who would
venture on to the premises for the first time. Don't be surprised or

discouraged if immediate reaction from some quarters is that the parish is fine as it is, *What was good enough for my parents and grandparents,* etc.! The emerging assessments of others around the table will, over time, have the desired effect of overcoming complacency and lingering Luddite tendencies.

> *There came a time when the risk to remain tight in the*
> *bud was more painful than the risk it took to blossom.*
> (Anais Nin)

From gatherings of both vestry and evangelism committee the streams of thought that emerge will likely be similar and, of course, subjective. Nonetheless this process will yield a valuable starting place.

It's possible that someone will have observed astutely: *I think we are all too close to the matter. How does a complete outsider react to being with us?* And that, of course, is really the crux of the issue. It will be addressed in Seed 11.

Growing Tip

The arrival of newcomers, whether they subsequently stayed or not, might be viewed as a means of securing feedback. However it is very likely that they will choose to not provide a frank objective assessment for reasons of tact and politeness. In any case, their coverage is likely to be limited.

Seed 11   **Objective Critique of the Parish**

You could seek out and commission an experienced grower of churches to visit, critically study the parish, document findings and recommendations, and brief the vestry (including a Q and A opportunity).

Commentary

We don't see things as they are; we see them as we are.
(wisdom attributed to several writers)

How does one locate the ideal person whom we'll call the commissioned visitor? Seed 8 provides one source of advice, but there are also your local clergy colleagues and your diocesan bishop.

Listen to advice and accept instruction, that you may
gain wisdom for the future.
(Proverbs 19.20)

One seeks a person who understands the ethos of our liturgical church but who can recognize shortcomings in its communications, operations, worship practices, programmatic aspects and its facilities. That the person is Episcopalian is less important than their church-growing background and their ability to cogently and objectively tell it like it is without sugar coatings and obfuscations.

Every branch that bears fruit he prunes
to make it bear more fruit.
(John 15.2)

Such consultation is best spelled out in a letter of understanding describing outputs, delivery schedule, and remuneration.

Of course, less-formal approaches will have value. Perhaps as a starting point, you might simply request a visit and descriptive report from a person you know, someone who is knowledgeable, observant, and objective.

In a time of drastic change it is the learners who in-
herit the future. The learned usually find themselves
equipped to live in a world that no longer exists.
(Eric Hoffer)

READER'S GROWING NOTES

Chapter 6

SEEDS FOR GROWTH IN GENERAL

Seed 12   **Referencing Hadaway's Work**

Encourage those in leadership positions within the parish to become familiar with the Hadaway reports [2, 3] on the Episcopal Church.

Commentary

There's much to be gained by you and the leadership team coming together to share reactions to this analysis. Typically, they can range from defensiveness to, *I've been saying that for years!* However, the overall achievement of such sharing is likely to be:

- a view of the parish from a new perspective
- a dispelling of complacency
- early recognition of improvements necessary
- realization of opportunities presenting themselves

See, I am making all things new.
(Rev. 21.5b)

Growing Tip

Over time, this collective review and sharing will assist the leadership team in relating to other parishioners the rationale for church-growing initiatives that are seen underway.

Seed 13   **A Cogent, Succinct-Yet-Inspiring Mission Statement**

Develop a mission* statement that supports your church-growing goals.

Commentary

Hadaway [2] stresses the *clarity of mission and purpose and the religious character of the congregation. Growing churches are clear about why they exist and what they should be doing. They do not grow because they have been at the corner of Elm Street and Main. They do not grow because they focus on long-term members. They grow because they understand their reason for being* [recall Archbishop William Temple] *and make sure they 'stick to their knitting'.*

In the author's experience, the creation or upgrading of the parish mission statement is best accomplished at a vestry retreat in a setting that encourages focused fresh thinking about key issues:

- as *sent out people,* how will we serve Christ?
- how does the surrounding community define our mission opportunities?
- what are its circumstances and needs? **
- for what other purposes does this congregation exist?
- our core values?

Mission statements of other progressive congregations may offer starting points for your deliberations but only that. The vestry needs to

---

* Mission, from the Latin missio = a sending out. See also the preamble to Seeds 61-64.
** Appendix 1 sheds light on this matter.

be fully invested in their own product. The intellectual struggle will be well worth it over the years to come.

Growing Tip

The mission statement serves as a principal tool because you will be able to draw attention to it again and again in the years that follow. To become most effective, it should figure strongly in the congregation's experiences. Consider some of the ways:

- at the worship-space entrance
- as masthead to weekly worship bulletins and regular newsletters
- as introductory information at the annual general meeting
- on your letter heading and literature promoting the parish
- and occasionally within the sermon

> As one wag remarked, *If you don't know where you are going, any road will get you there.*
> (Folk wisdom, source unknown)

Seed 14 **You—Visible Symbol**

Recall the seed sown long ago.

Commentary

Your role as symbol was sown at ordination when, with that *take-my-yoke-upon-you* rite of passage, you first donned the clerical collar. Henceforth, all seeing it would sense the presence of the church in the community. Out there you travel back and forth endlessly doing the tasks of your ministry. Out there the collar announces that the church is alive and active in our midst.

So we are ambassadors for Christ, since God
is making his appeal through us; …
(2 Corinthians 5.20a)

Seed 15 **"Personality" of the Parish Office**

Assess whether the present parish-office setup adequately supports church growth.

Commentary

Prepare the way of the Lord,
(Mark 1.3)

As nerve center for the congregation, the office is ground zero for church-growing endeavors and those staffing it are frequently in the vanguard of efforts. Whether it is experienced in person, or by telephone, recorded message, fax or regular correspondence, the office presents a personality. What do you gauge that personality to be? At its best, the office is the warm welcome of the congregation, its smile, its helpfulness, its encouragement, its patience, and its keeper of promises. At its worst … well, let's not go there but move on to consider the office as image. Does the office present a bright, cheerful, uncluttered, efficient work space or a jaded portrayal of bygone eras and practices? These aspects deserve early remedial attention as you undertake growing your church.

Seed 16   **Communications Equipment**

Evaluate the adequacy of communications equipment for the in-creased demands that will be placed upon it and make the necessary improvements.

Commentary

Communications are vitally important for the congregation that would evangelize. Correspondingly, the growing church will learn to place ever-increasing demands upon communications equipment of all kinds and in all places–worship space, parish hall, music room, nursery, classrooms and church offices. What if the general budget cannot handle the cost? Blessedly, the pricing structure of such items make them ideal candidates for gifting and the use of Seeds 77 and 78, discussed later.

Seed 17   **Motivational Speakers**

Periodically, have guest speakers address the congregation, providing in-spiration and encouragement for church-growing work that lies ahead.

Commentary

> *Judas and Silas, who were themselves prophets, said*
> *much to encourage and strengthen the believers.*
> (Acts 15.32)

Seeds 7 and 8 offer the means of identifying suitable speakers.

Years ago, our teenage daughter's bedroom sported a poster showing a kitten dangling precariously from the branch of a tree. The caption read,

> *Hang in there, God isn't finished with you yet.*

It seemed to summarize Holy Scripture, its challenge to the Church and every member. Your guest speakers can help convey God's endless hope and promise.

The following nineteen Seeds* address the numerous ways by which, actively or passively, you can draw your parish to the attention of prospective visitors. Such persons may be established residents of the area or have settled there just recently. They also may be *out-of-towners* if your parish is located near such features as recreational areas, cultural centers, places of historic interest, national or state parks, and coastal regions.

> *Do not neglect to show hospitality to strangers, for by do-*
> *ing that some have entertained angels without knowing it.*
> (Hebrews 13:2)

Seed 18　　　　　　**"The Episcopal Church Welcomes You"**

Ideally, the long-established Episcopal-Church welcoming signs should commence a block or two away from the church facilities although it's noted that some municipalities impose restrictions in this regard.

---

* Chapter 7 adds one more, the Vacation Bible School.

Commentary

From sea to shining sea — the red, white and blue welcoming sign in towns and cities across our nation has been one of the wisest public-relations campaigns that our denomination ever mounted. Brand recognition? Not in the realms of the golden arches, but it's well up there! Suppliers may be accessed via the internet.

Seed 19 **Parish Web Site**

Establish and maintain a parish web site.

Commentary

Some prospective newcomers will seek out your web site and the more actively it is maintained the more effective an evangelizing tool it will be. Viewers of the web page will span a spectrum of age groups, needs, and interests; select your scenes of parish life accordingly.

As with all publicity communications, give very clear instructions to locate the church facilities, a map always being helpful. Also, set worship times visibly on the home page without the need to scroll down or click. Congregations with a website are *most likely to grow* says Hadaway [2] and, conversely, *Congregations that would oppose a web site are very unlikely to have experienced growth.* In similar fashion, the parish may find Facebook helpful.

Seed 20   **Facilities Sharing**

If you are not doing so already, consider making your splendid worship space available for public meetings, concerts, choir festivals etc.., and likewise your classrooms for Twelve-Step and other similar programs.

Commentary

For too many in our increasingly secular society, the thought of making that rare appearance in a sacred setting can stir up sundry phobias and discomfort. The more the church setting is experienced by the people of your district, the more comfortable they may become, and the better will be your prospects of evangelizing among them.

Seed 21   **Bumper Stickers**

Make available in quantity the bumper sticker, *The Episcopal Church Welcomes You* and encourage parishioners to place it on their vehicles.

Commentary

This is another of those several instances where you, the vestry, and the evangelism committee lead best by example.

Seed 22 **Chamber of Commerce**

Take out membership and use the resources of the local Chamber of Commerce if you have one.

Commentary

Membership may enable you to place the Episcopal welcoming sign on the Chamber's highway billboard, at the approaches to town amidst those of Rotary, Kiwanis, etc.

Local offices of the Chamber of Commerce typically have displays of literature about local organizations for the benefit of newcomers and visitors. Use this opportunity to feature details of the parish.

Seed 23 **Hotel Notice Boards**

Hotels and motels are yet other possibilities for displaying information regarding the parish.

Let us go to the house of the Lord!
(Psalm 122.1)

Seed 24   **Newcomer Association etc.**

Newcomer Associations or similar groups often provide people settling in the area with a package of literature. Membership can give you access to such advertising opportunities.

Seed 25   **Visitor Centers**

If you are located in a popular tourist destination, the respective visitor centers typically offer the opportunity to display details of your worship schedule.

Seed 26   **Yellow Pages**

Most churches still employ the Yellow Pages to connect with newcomers and visitors to town. However, for some of these people Google is providing the new (web-site) directory.

Seed 27   **Local Newspaper**

The Church Directory page of the local newspaper's weekend edition remains a helpful advertising device. Special events in the parish (bishop's visitation for example) written up for the local newspaper, enhanced by a photograph, are yet further inducements for the locals to check you out and may be treated as a free press release. But, for the un-churched reader out there, the most compelling articles are accounts of ordinary people journeying in faith to overcome loss, adversity, frailty, and fear. Every congregation has them. We are a people of the Gospel and the Gospel is about giving hope. Such accounts can impart hope to those who need it most, the disillusioned, the despairing; all those who are down and seek a way of getting up. *I am the way, and the truth, and the life* Jesus says. (John 14.6a)

Seed 28   **Literature Box**

For people checking out the parish *after hours*, draw attention to available literature concerning congregational life.

Commentary

The clear-plastic *Take One* box typically used by realtors is a convenient means of making materials available. Set up near the church entrance, it says much about your congregation's unfailing desire to connect with the stranger.

At this point, it's necessary to set the stage for the Seed that follows and to do so with Jesus' exhortation to his followers on service to others. (Matthew 5.14-16)

> *You are the light of the world. A city built on a hill cannot be hid. No one after lighting a lamp puts it under a bushel basket, but on a lampstand, and it gives light*

*to all in the house. In the same way let your light shine
before others, so that they may see your good works
and give glory to your Father in heaven.*

Dopp [4] writes of two types of church, the old chapel church (OCC) and the emerging missionary church (EMC). *One church is self-centered; the other is Christ-centered. Survival is the concern of the self-centered; mission and ministry is the calling of the Christ-centered.*

He goes on. *The old chapel church is the place where an individual prays; the emerging missionary church is where people pray together and then go out into the world to do the work of the body of Christ.*

The OCC is in the final days of its life cycle, writes Dopp. *It is a holy decline, because God has the need for a new mission. The EMC must become the new way we exercise our faith.*

It's evident that people are drawn to the EMC rather than the OCC because of the high regard in which service to the community is generally held. Consequently, if yours is a congregation active in outreach, do not be bashful, do not be reticent. Rather, use available opportunities to *let your light shine before others* within the local community. Seed 29 speaks to this very necessary communication.

Seed 29 **Maximizing Outreach Visibility**

Use all opportunities to make the local community aware of your efforts to extend the kingdom of God.

Commentary

Perhaps your church supports or even operates one or more services to the needy of your region. The following is a sample of congregational initiatives.

- food bank
- thrift store
- family support services
- shelter for the homeless
- auxiliary hospital services
- Thanksgiving/Christmas food boxes
- soup kitchen
- clothing assistance
- prison ministry
- victim-offender reconciliation

Or perhaps you organize fund-raising events to support local charities, or make space freely available to the various 12-step programs or English-language instruction for example.

For reasons just presented, the EMC ethos of your congregation is one that has the potential to attract the seeker. This potential is realized if you systematically increase the local community's awareness of your outreach. Some suggestions on how to achieve this are:

- a photograph and article in the local newspaper on occasions of *good news* and milestone events in the life of your various outreach programs
- illustration of these programs on your website
- presenting details of your programs on *showing-the-flag* occasions of Seeds 19, 22, 24, 30 and 32

Coordinating responsibility for this Seed is best placed in hands of the evangelism committee.

Seed 30   **Farmer's Market**

With farmer's markets increasing in popularity, having a stall for your parish is a means of informing local people of your presence and programs through your banner, signs, handout literature and, most importantly, your team's personal sharing and enthusiasm.

Commentary

What to sell? Parishioner-baked goods have been shown to work well. Beverages offer another solution. But the selling is merely incidental. The overriding consideration is that you are letting the local community know that you exist and that you invite them to explore the spiritually enriching experiences of attending your church. As a further consideration, why not invite the Market to meet on the parish parking lot?

Seed 31   **The All-Purpose Banner**

Working with your local signs-and-banners store, design and purchase an all-weather banner, something on the order of 10 feet or perhaps even longer.

Commentary

A good working relationship with this store is a notable feature of the congregation that grows. You will call upon its services in several ways over the years.

This particular banner proclaims the key slogan of your parish evangelism program. It might be arrived at from your parish mission statement or the parish profile statement of goals but, more than likely, it will evolve afresh from the deliberations of the evangelism committee. "Friendly, Welcoming in Christ" is just one example of what might emblazon the entry to your church facilities or be flown on the occasion of Seeds 20, 30, 32, 35, 36 and 72.

> *May we... in the name of our God set up our banners.*
> (Psalm 20.5)

Seed 32　　　　**Joining the Parade**

Take your invitation downtown.

Commentary

America loves its annual parade. Down Main Street it comes. Fire engine's klaxon. Cheering crowds. Marching bands. Antique cars bearing Parade Marshals. Children on decorated bicycles. Bemedaled veterans. Boy scouts. Clowns tossing candy to the sidewalks. Girls' ballet school. Trucks of little soccer players. Prancing percherons. 4-H display. And there, amidst it all, the local Episcopal Church.

What a great day! What a great way to *show the flag*. And what fun it was for the congregation to decorate that flatbed float with flowers and bunting around the parishioner tableau and instrumentalists, all under the huge banner extending a welcome. Happy faces. Come and join us.

Seed 33   **Inviting by Telephone Campaign**

For a dynamic evangelizing campaign, recruit and coach a telephone team. With a standard message and approach, and prayerful preparation, tackle a specific district of the region at a time, say of a thousand or two households making use of a reverse directory, i.e. one listing names and numbers street by street.

Commentary

Such blocks of phoning might be scheduled in weeks leading up to Easter Sunday, Pentecost or Christmas so that the invitation to worship coincides with Spirit-filled splendors. Those expressing interest in attending are best sent a brief packet of information concerning the parish. The power of the project is that its person-to-person communication and not something mailed or simply left on the doorstep (although such measures do have some value).

Of course, some invitees will respond that they already attend a church, thank you. The majority of others will turn down the invitation. Yet, blessedly, some seed will fall on fertile soil. Remember, those who declined cannot erase the fact that, perhaps for the first time, someone (your parish) invited them to church. Who knows what the future will bring and the change in heart that unforeseen events bring about. The seed can grow silently for quite some time.

One substantially positive side effect of such campaigns is that parishioners, some of whom probably have never invited anyone to church in their entire lives, discover that they can. Furthermore, there was real joy in doing so. They grow spiritually in that newly found ability and will probably exercise it again and again. The anxiety barrier has been breached.

A very notable newcomer from our telephoning campaigning was Nancy*. Small in stature but large in presence, frail in body yet strong in spirit, Nancy soon made it known that she wanted lots of other people to experience what she'd felt on entering the parish. Joining the Evangelism Committee, she eventually became its Chairperson. It was Nancy who conceived of our Farmer's Market initiative (Seed 30) and championed our Joining the Parade (Seed 32).

> *…, I was a stranger and you welcomed me.*
> (Matt. 25.35b)

Seed 34 **Ride Sharing**

Recruit a network of volunteers from across the parish who, as needed, will offer a ride to and from church.

Commentary

Inevitably, there are people who would be part of your congregation but have a need for transportation. You will require a small coordinator team to bring about this *loving-your-neighbor* service which, when operating, should be mentioned in your advertising efforts.

---

* Nancy was *different*. In dress, manner, and speech she stood out. To bring people into our Church, rector and congregation must increasingly address society's diversity. See Appendix 1.

Seed 35   **Inviting a Friend**

Plan for an annual or more frequent "Invite-a-Friend" Sunday as a means of stimulating all-year-around efforts.

Commentary

> *Go home to your friends, and tell them how*
> *much the Lord has done for you, and what mercy*
> *he has shown you.*
> (Mark 5.19)

Ideally, parishioners are so excited about their church that they want to invite a friend every Sunday. If not, there's more work to do on the quality of preaching, liturgy, music, parish life etc. That said, with suitable advance publicity, this day should be a special time of recognizing and celebrating the newcomer's presence and the post-worship reception is a grand time to do this. The pertinence of the lectionary and the preaching it affords may influence your selection of the Sunday. Music and prayers can also reflect the theme of the day.

Hadaway reports [2], *As other studies have shown, the primary first connect with a congregation is through a pre-existing relationship with someone who is already involved.* He adds, *Where 'a lot' of members are involved in recruitment, 52% of congregations are growing. By contrast, where very few members are involved in recruitment, hardly any of those congregations are experiencing growth.*

In his Gospel, John (1.43ff) tells of Philip freshly called by Jesus with a simple *Follow me.* Shortly thereafter Philip persuasively shares newly found faith with a skeptical Nathanael. *Come and see,* says Philip, forerunner of all who would invite a friend to church or to attend the ALPHA course, for example.

Seed 36   **ALPHA**

Among the ways of bringing people into Christ's church, the worldwide ALPHA program is a standout evangelizing tool.

Commentary

Originating within and for the Church of England, ALPHA now has a multi-denominational following in the USA and across the world. Googling ALPHA reveals that two million people in the USA have taken the course which is also to be found operating in over 160 other countries. Worldwide, the total attendance has reached 16 million. What it is and how to offer it is detailed online to such an extent that it will not be echoed here.

With the experience borne of running the ALPHA program on four occasions, the author sees it as a powerful Christianizing force not only in the experiences of outsiders who attend but also in the lives of the parish team staffing it.

Of this Gospel I have become a servant...
(Eph. 3.7a)

The discerning power of these round-table gatherings of seeker and initiated, week by week, was foretold in Rom. 15.14, 1 Cor. 14.31, and Eph. 4.15.

Seed 37   **Your Title**

In all your efforts to connect with prospective newcomers, give some consideration as to what you call yourself.

Commentary

If you asked ten people on Main Street, *What is a rector?* you'd surely be surprised if one response came close. Doubtless, they would do much better if you had asked, *What is a pastor?* There's a lesson in communication to be learned here. The newcomer and notably the uninitiated will find it easier to connect with you the "pastor," at least at first. Remember, page 531 of the Book of Common Prayer [1] has the bishop express this at your ordination to the priesthood.

> *Now you are called to work as a <u>pastor</u>, priest, and*
> *teacher together with your bishop and*
> *fellow presbyters.*
> [Author's underlining]

Likewise from page 534, the bishop called upon the Lord to make you *a faithful pastor...* Following Saint Paul's example (1 Cor. 9.19-22), this accommodating approach can be helpful in early communication with prospective church members.

What do newcomers encounter upon approaching and entering your church facilities? What does it feel like to be strangers* in your midst?

---

* So often central figures in Biblical stories of faith.

With possibly little or no experience of it, how will they engage in the worship? Will they struggle and succeed? Or will they fail and be frustrated? The church that would grow needs to make this visit memorable and uplifting but also as reassuring, comfortable and pleasant as possible with the earnest hope that the visitors will return. How does the parish bring this outcome about? Seeds 37 - 54 point the way.

Then let us no more pass judgment on one another, but
rather decide never to put a stumbling block or hin-
drance in the way of another.
(Romans 14.13)

Seed 38   **Appearance Matters**

Every picture tells a story.

So endeavor to maintain *curb appeal* and indeed all aspects of the facilities as attractive and functional as the Building and Grounds Committee and the budget can make it.

Commentary

Does this place look loved? Is parishioner pride evident? Success in growing the church will be strongly influenced by the immediate perceptions of first-time visitors.

Periodic parish-wide calls for Saturday-morning spruce ups worked wonders for us and the luncheon fellowship that followed was always a strong inducement to turn up.

Seed 39   **First-Time-Visitor Parking**

If your church is served by a parking lot, set aside several most-favorably-located parking spaces with the sign, *For First-time Visitors* or *Guest Parking*. If your parish has only street parking, similarly try to accomplish reserved parking for their benefit.

Commentary

By your action you are expressing that you are honored by the newcomers' presence. Their visit is special. After all, bringing people into the Church is a primary reason for the congregation's existence.

Seed 40   **Helpful Signs**

Install a coherent system of signs around the buildings so that first-time visitors can readily locate key facilities: restrooms, worship space, nursery, Sunday-school rooms, music room, parish hall, church office, pastor's office, etc.

Commentary

Computer graphics have made the production of signage fast and economical. Once again, your local signs-and-banners store can provide for your needs. Just ensure that you employ only terms that the stranger will readily understand.

Seed 41   **Inviting- Church Posters**

Explore internet access to sources of posters that express the concepts of inviting a friend and welcoming the stranger.

Commentary

A rich variety of eye-catching posters are available which, placed around the facilities, can, over time, foster a welcoming, sharing attitude on the part of parishioners. Furthermore, such posters convey the reassuring message to the newcomer, *I am most welcome here.*

Seed 42   **Greeter's Table**

If your church architecture permits it, staff a greeter's table near the entrance to the worship space.

Commentary

> *Welcome one another, therefore, just as Christ has welcomed you, for the glory of God.*
> (Rom. 15.7)

A growing church is best served by a greeter team working in parallel to the traditional usher team. Simply put, the ushers' tasks take place within the worship space while the greeters' work mostly occurs prior to the parishioner's/visitor's entry (two exceptions to this will be touched on later).

Where you are fortunate enough to have a suitably large and all-weather gathering area just outside the worship space, the greeter's table can perform several important functions. Information displayed there tells of current and forthcoming events in the life of the church. There are sign-up sheets and, most notably, the guest book. First-time visitors are encouraged to provide their name and address, the significance of which is presented in subsequent seeds. If they add the telephone number and email address, that is additionally helpful.

The skilled greeter is watchful for a visitor's uncertainty and, with a smile, ready to assist as necessary: *Is there a nursery? A Sunday school for my children? The restrooms? May the children rejoin us at the Holy Communion?*

Hospitality its maxim, the greeter team strives to make people feel at ease and welcomed.

Growing Tip

Teenagers and even pre-teenagers may make excellent ambassadors for the parish and speak volumes about the congregation's supportive attitude toward young people, an aspect readily absorbed by young-family newcomers.

Periodic meetings of the greeters serve to educate and motivate and provide a forum in which to resolve any new issues that crop up.

Seed 43   **Paper Name Tag**

At the greeters table, provide everyone with a boldly-written, adhesive, paper name tag.

Commentary

A congregation that truly aims to welcome and incorporate the newcomer must grow to accept the practice of sporting a name tag: *Hello! I'm ......*

Now I know that some congregations prepare and display durable name plates for the members in the hope that each will actually seek out their plate and wear it (and subsequently return it). But do they? And where does that leave the newcomer/visitor? A three-tier system emerges: 1) some wear, 2) some do not and 3) at best, the newcomer gets an ad hoc tag. It's desirable that name tags do not segregate, defining "outsiders" and "insiders". The better system is that name tags are disposable (and cheap), the sort typically worn at social functions. "Oldcomers" and "newcomers" alike have this written out for them at the greeters table with a thick felt pen so that it serves its real purpose i.e. it's readily readable, a yard or two away.

The greeters table thus becomes a great setting for connecting and reconnecting, putting names to faces, and learning how people are faring in their lives (and hence a source of information important to pastoral ministry).

Seed 44   **Your Presence with the Greeters**

Your presence near the greeters table prior to services may be an important part of growing a church.

Commentary

Sunday morning is *clergy prime time* — so emphasized the rector of the parish in which I received seminarian field training. Use it for maximum effectiveness I was told.

With church-growing efforts underway, time spent near the greeters table is most effective. It enables the greeters to have you meet the newcomers, the second of hopefully numerous contacts they will make that day. Your presence and actions underscore the importance of being an inviting congregation. In the eyes of parishioners, you are their prime example, their flag bearer, their champion of the cause. Additionally, it's another means of you staying in touch with parishioners, their changing situations, and needs.

Should you find that the resulting intake of information is greater than you could possibly retain, don't hesitate to have a warden or vestry member or evangelism committee member at your side discreetly making notes.

All this presumes that you would feel comfortable in this role. If that's not the case, consider asking a warden to take it on.

Seed 45   **Worship's Draw**

Make it your aim to always lead worship in such a manner that the uninitiated newcomer feels comfortable, included, and readily able to follow along.

Commentary

> *Welcome those who are weak in faith…*
> (Rom. 14.1a)

All worship affords opportunity for evangelism. This is especially true when the unchurched attend baptisms, weddings, and funerals or the special services of Christmas and Eastertide. Moved by the Spirit, they come out of personal desire or respect, or to please family or friends. Whatever the reason, hold fast to the words of Saint Francis of

Assisi, *Always preach the Gospel and, when necessary, use words.* It's your actions that will speak volumes.

Yes, of course, existing members do not need the degree of guidance that you are now providing. They are well versed in the shifts and changes in our venerable worship forms. But, through your communications over time, they have come to understand and accept the new approach for the simple reason that, *We are now an evangelizing congregation intent on bringing others to Christ.*

Seed 46   **Newcomer-Friendly Bulletins**

Consider extending preparation of worship bulletins to embrace as much of the service as is practical.

Commentary

Even the experienced worshiper will find this helpful while the uninitiated is relieved of anxiety and free to focus on what really matters.

The extended bulletin also gives you flexibility to incorporate songs and hymns not found in the music books located in the pew rack. Furthermore, it's a means of enriching the worship experience by the use of other liturgies from time to time.

Seed 47   **Capturing Scripture's Power**

Strive for the most meaning-filled, passion-capturing reading of scripture that your lector team can grow to achieve.

Commentary

> *It ain't what you say; it's the way that you say it…*

Like others before me, I take liberties with the 1939 song by Melvin Oliver and James Young to make an important point.

Worship in the Episcopal Church has a powerful component that is rarely given the care and attention that it warrants. We are a church of scripture, not a snippet here and there, chosen at the whim of the pastor, but a scholarly-assembled lectionary set of four passages, two from the Hebrew Scriptures and two from the New Testament.

In its origination and early application, the scriptural message was delivered with passion borne of understanding and commitment to every word and nuance. Your goal is surely to have that scripture read so that it comes alive in your midst, to light a fire in the hearts of all who hear it and especially in the hearts of those newcomers you are trying to reach with the Good News.

> *Indeed, the word of God is living and active,*
> *sharper than a two-edged sword,…*
> (Hebr. 4.12a)

Your goal is surely to have the listener reach a depth of understanding and empowerment they have never experienced before, to feel the electricity in the air and see the light in the worshiper's eyes when they finally release pent-up breath and respond *Thanks be to God*. So, how are your lectors performing this potentially powerful portion of our worship? What are the congregation's faces saying? Did the eyes light up or did they glaze over?

I recommend that you lead periodic workshops for your lector team complete with handout notes on what good preparation and delivery entails. Over time, be watchful for those in the congregation with the gift of good speaking ability (incidentally a grand way of incorporating the newcomer). Endeavor to recruit them, expanding the ranks and reading quality of your lector team, explaining what you are seeking and working with them in practice sessions against the backdrop of your guidance notes. Of course, the clergy's reading of the Gospel should demonstrate the striving for quality that is underway.

Saint Paul's pastoral words to Timothy (1 Tim. 4.13-15) have uncanny bearing on the above.

> *Until I arrive, give attention to the public reading of scripture, to exhortation, to teaching. Do not neglect the gift that is in you, which was given to you through prophecy with the laying on of hands by the council of the elders. Put these things into practice; devote yourself to them, so that all may see your progress.*

Growing Tip

Human nature being what it is, some lectors may declare *I don't need that*. From the listener's perspective, ironically, they are often the ones who need improvement most. For pastoral considerations, sometimes all you can do is work around them hoping that the improving quality of reading by others will prompt them to put in greater effort. Teenagers and young adults may excel in adapting to what you are aiming for.

In time, God may smile on your efforts and send you a high school teacher well versed in coaching speech and drama skills to whom you can delegate this important responsibility.

Seed 48 **Music's Powerful Influence**

Think long and hard about the choice of music your congregation is invited to sing, how it is accompanied, and how the growth of the parish is thereby helped or hindered.

Commentary

Hadaway [2] reports *that congregations that describe their worship as joyful are more likely to experience growth.* This was based upon the national survey question, *How well does 'it is joyful' describe your worship service with the largest attendance?* Those congregations that responded *strongly agree* were three times more likely to grow than those who responded *disagree.* So how does a congregation primarily experience joy? In a word, music.

Singing is a very empowering part of worship and, for some, the most empowering. Wikipedia's section on "church music" helpfully illustrates these points and reminds us that Augustine of Hippo observed, *To sing once is to pray twice.* This same section goes on to note, *music has the evangelical purpose of attracting those whose enthusiasm for religious matters is not sufficient on its own.* So reassess your time of song. Is organ the preferred or only instrument? What place is there for other instruments?* What do the singers' faces tell you? The voices? The body language? Is there fervor in the renderings? And the key question, what is a newcomer likely to witness, feel, and retain from the experience?

Do you rely solely upon The Hymnal 1982 [4]? Despite its unassailable scholarship, the beauty of most melodies and careful adherence to

---

* An Appendix 1 diversity issue.

Anglican Theology**, too many of its lyrics fail to connect with and speak to today's worshipers, and particularly younger people. How is our increasingly secular and biblically illiterate society to comprehend and be nourished spiritually by lyrics penned in the archaic phrasing of bygone centuries and using metaphors of scripture recognized by the few?

> *We put no obstacle in any one's way, so that no fault*
> *may be found with our ministry...*
> (2 Corinthians 6.3 RSV)

When singing becomes rote and emotions are not stirred by resonant identification with words, then its potential spiritual empowerment is lost and we are the poorer for it.

Blessedly, the entire Christian spectrum seems to have been stimulated by the surge in musical creativity unleashed by Vatican II in the early 1960's. Today, there are many theologically sound sources of music with which to supplement The Hymnal. Their readily understood, spiritually engaging words and evangelizing power has long been recognized within the movements of Cursillo, Faith Alive, ALPHA and, of course, the churches that grow.

> *... be filled with the Spirit, as you sing psalms and*
> *hymns and spiritual songs among yourselves,...*
> (Eph. 5.18-19)

Let's assume that you have identified a number of the most spiritually uplifting pieces of music sung in American churches today. You sense that they will add joy to the worship and seek to make them part of the congregation's repertoire. This is done best over an extended period of time by occasionally introducing a lighthearted teaching moment prior to formally opening the service. In my parish, the Minister of Music would take the lead, firstly playing and singing the melody, then having

---

** However, how much theology does the singer really need to absorb during this hallowed time of praise to God?

the choir render a portion. At this stage, the congregation was invited to try it; this they did enthusiastically. At its appointed place in the service, the new song was sung with evident pride in the achievement. *Sing to the Lord a new song...,* wrote prophet Isaiah (Isaiah 42.10a). So we did, regularly, and with an emphasis on readily understood lyrics, memorable melodies, and the total effect of joy.

On an annual basis, the parish purchased licensing rights enabling us to print the new music in the worship bulletin.

Of course, even singing a new song will bring out the naysayer. I well recall an older woman of the congregation exiting the church doors at the service close and informing me that, *the music had reached an all-time low!* It hurt! Ironically, the overwhelmingly favorable response to measures you will take to grow your church never seems to counter the impact of the isolated negative reaction. But I'll say more about naysaying and resistance to change *In Closing.*

Seed 49   **Music as Ministry**

Reassess expectations of the person leading your music program as well as position title.

Commentary

Music is such a powerful component of growing a church that the increasingly vital role of the person leading this program should be foreseen and allowed for. Most likely you will expect this person to demonstrate:

- knowledge and acceptance of diverse musical genres
- competence with both piano and organ and appreciation of other instrumental enrichment

- good communication and teaching skills
- an outgoing, friendly personality
- a prayerful, pastoral disposition

Furthermore, you will come to expect the person to:

- contribute to your regular staff meetings
- research and select music to your general guidelines
- address any licensing requirements
- direct choirs and instrumentalists
- provide some of them with mentoring and even pastoral support as the need arises
- alert you to pastoral concerns requiring your attention
- lead *teaching moments* as the congregation is introduced to new music
- play a role in welcoming the stranger and recruiting choir members and instrumentalists
- become musical collaborator to Vacation Bible School and the growing range of activities of the Children, Youth and Family Ministry
- work with you in planning special events
- interface with organizations seeking to use your worship space for musical activities

Let's think about the position title. A title creates expectations. That's generally understood. A title will create expectations from the congregation but, most importantly, in the mind and motivation of the holder. Job-limiting titles such as Organist and Choir Director no longer fit. They've been outgrown. For whether lay or ordained, this person has become Minister of Music, your close collaborator in evangelism.

That much has been said here on the matter of music serves to underscore its importance in growing a congregation.

Seed 50 **Memento of Newcomer Visit**

During the worship, at the Passing of the Peace, greeters discreetly locate newcomers in the pews to present them with a memento of their visit.

Commentary

The evangelism committee may suggest a suitable memento perhaps one unique to your location. However, in the author's parish, the chosen memento was a small olive-wood cross purchased in bulk from workshops at Bethlehem in the Holy Land. Parishioner volunteers fashioned it with a decorative cord that it might be worn around the neck and inscribed it in fine hand, with the name of the parish. In the enclosing plastic packet was a note of welcome that explained the gift's origins.

Googling *Holy Land Olive Wood Crosses* provides access to the Arab Christian suppliers. Their service has been excellent.

Seed 51 **Holy Communion Guidance**

In regard to the Holy Communion portion of the service, ideally the bulletin will provide guidance on how to receive the sacrament so that visiting uninitiated worshippers might feel comfortable with what takes place.

Commentary

Since baptisms, weddings and funerals are special opportunities for evangelism; this guidance regarding the Holy Communion is best expressed by you. Furthermore, you do well to include the observation that it is Christ's invitation to his table and not merely that of our particular denomination.

Seed 52 **Common Cup Concerns**

Address the issue of the common cup with care and especially as it affects the newcomer.

Commentary

As a society, we have become excessively concerned with cleanliness and disinfection. Advertising media would have us in a state of hygiene hysteria. So, what is the uninitiated worshiper to think on witnessing the chalice passing from mouth to mouth with only a cursory touch of the purificator? There is surely a comfort issue here and one to not ignore if church growth is your goal.

Several actions might be taken to alleviate concerns. As a start, you could ensure that the linen purificator is shaken out of its tightly ironed state to maximize its effectiveness. Your bulletin could point out that it is sufficient to receive the bread alone and that, if the arms are crossed, the chalice will not be offered. If it's your custom to use wafers, the bulletin could point out that intinction (also explained) is acceptable. If, alternatively, your practice is to offer bread, you might consider switching to special-recipe flat bread that may be intincted without crumbling into the chalice.

Growing Tip

In any congregation, there is that small group of people for whom baking the special-recipe bread is a cherished task.

Incidentally, as you distribute the bread at the Holy Communion, those boldly written name tags will, over time, assist you in learning people's names, a very helpful aspect of growing your church.

Seed 53 **Those Seven Introductions**

At the close of the worship, greeter team members are alert to offer any further assistance to newcomers.

Commentary

Particularly important is the making of appropriate introductions at the coffee hour over in the parish hall, the commonly accepted rule of thumb being that newcomers should visit with at least seven people to feel that they have been recognized and accepted. The congregation is privileged to extend God's hospitality.

> *All guests who present themselves are to be*
> *welcomed as Christ for he himself will say: "I*
> *was a stranger and you welcomed me."*
> (Abridged Edition of the Rule of St. Benedict 1980,
> chapter 53, p. 103f)

Seed 54   **Hello, I'm Mary and this is…**

Encourage your flock to make a practice of extending a welcoming hand to the visitor.

Commentary

Periodically, through preaching and newsletter writings, convey the effectiveness of this simple action in welcoming the stranger and how important it is for all to play their part. The mantra for this ministry is surely: *It's our job. It's our joy. It's the reason we are here.*

Christ claiming us as friends (John 15. 14-15) and loving us all as we are is captured so well in Hymn 603 [5]. Most importantly, stanza 4 conveys Christ's expectation that we extend that friendship in welcoming others.

> *Thus freely loved, though fully known,*
> *may I in Christ be free to welcome*
> *and accept his own as Christ accepted me.*
> (Taken from "When Christ was lifted from the Earth" by Brian Wren
> © 1973 Hope Publishing Company, Carol Stream, 1L 60188. All right
> reserved. Used by permission.)

In this regard I'll share something personal. My wife and I, with our three young children, came to the USA in October, 1967. On our first Sunday in Glenview, Illinois, we attended the local Episcopal Church. Why there? Because back in England our local curate, Wilfred Gash, had prepped us saying *that's our lot in America.* Our reception at Saint David's still remains the "gold standard" for what congregations might set out to be and do as evangelists. There were introductions and conversations galore at the coffee hour (several of which resulted in invitations to homes over the coming weeks). To cap it all, the rector, Gordon Lyall, and his wife invited us over to the rectory for brunch. That memorable morning marked the start of our many happy years of life and ministry within the Episcopal Church.

Would that all the Lord's people were prophets
and that the Lord would put his spirit on them.
(Num. 11.29)

Seed 55   **Monday's Follow-Up**

Use Mondays to follow up with the guest book and other visitor information gleaned the previous day.

Commentary

To newcomers residing locally, send out a personal letter from the pastor/rector (you judge). Typically, this might express delight at their visit, the offer to provide any information they might seek, and the hope that they might continue to worship with you. To visitors from out of town, the letter might merely convey your pleasure at their coming and the hope that they might return some time.

Hadaway [2] points out those *congregations that follow-up on visitors through mail, phone calls, emails, personal visits, mailed materials, etc. are the most likely to grow.*

Seed 56   **The PIE Program**

Within a few days of the local newcomer's visit, the evangelism committee arranges delivery to their residence of an item of baked goods together with a note of welcome from the congregation.

Commentary

I believe this concept originated at Trinity Church, Sacramento, California and was known as the PIE program (Parishioners Involved in Evangelism). PIE volunteers, under the auspices of the committee, are careful to make their visit as brief and non-pressuring as possible. From the parish freezer, the volunteer selects a previously prepared baked item, the loving output of others in the program.

Seed 57   **Celebrating Newcomer Visits**

Publish weekly in the worship bulletin the names of visitors who readily shared this information at the previous Sunday's worship.

Commentary

Of course, some visitors may convey a desire for privacy and this should be respected. Most will not, however. It's of value that the congregation's attention be drawn repeatedly to the aspect of welcoming the stranger and especially to success in doing so. Morale over the long haul is a key consideration.

Seed 58   **Newcomer Incorporation**

With little delay, invite newcomers to participate in a lay ministry.

Commentary

This powerful expression of *you are part of us* is a time-tested means of incorporating them. Yet again, participation feeds commitment. Your staff meeting and that of the evangelism committee provide settings in which to explore suitable invitations.

Seed 59   **Round-Table Communication**

Over time, progressively replace those traditional long tables in the parish hall with modern engineered circular tables that seat eight to ten people.

Commentary

Communication is of particular importance in the congregation that seeks to grow. Consider all those occasions of fellowship, education, reception and formal discussion. Consider the needs of Cursillo, Faith Alive, ALPHA, and Via Media. Ask yourself, which table setting fosters the greater eye-to-eye communication, all-round participation, sharing and openness.

The perfect illustration of improving communications can be set by introducing the use of a large round table top for vestry meetings and committee gatherings. Most parishes have handy people who can fashion this from two good-quality, veneered plywood boards, 4 x 8 feet in size and ¾ inch thick. Piano-hinged down the middle and given several coats of varnish, the result is a handsome economical top that can overlay those old-fashioned rectangular tables.

Seed 60　　　　　　　　**Fellowship Breakfasts**

Consider having between-services breakfasts in the parish hall throughout the year at, say, monthly intervals.

> *Contribute to the needs of the saints; extend*
> *hospitality to strangers.*
> (Rom. 12.13)

Commentary

Apart from their general community-building value, such gatherings achieve the following:

- they complement parishioners' invite-a-friend efforts
- they further the integration of recent newcomers
- they unify attendees of different worship services making for a more cohesive congregation
- they provide another setting for special announcements, award ceremonies, program presentations, etc.

In this preamble, ground is broken for Seeds 61-62, and perhaps also 63-64, by addressing the reality that those baptized into Christ were given a mission (Latin missio = a sending out). Your congregation is a *sent* people.

As the Father has sent me, so I send you
(John 20.21b)

....and you will be my witnesses...
(Acts 1.8)

And now Father, send us out to do the work you have given us to do, to love and serve you as faithful witness of Christ our Lord (Book of Common Prayer [1], The Holy Eucharist, Rite Two).

The congregation will constantly need to be made aware that as the baptized, as *the sent*, and as the Ministers of the Church; they are all involved in evangelism, in drawing others to the Good News of God in Christ.

Thus in preaching, teaching, and other communications over time, it's vitally important that you convey this reality. In doing so, you have splendid opportunity and illustration provided by seeds 29, 30, 32-36, 42, 53, 54, 56, 60, 66 and 72.

Lastly, bear in mind that every occasion of worship offers a time of *sending*.

Seed 61   **Reliving the Baptismal Covenant**

The congregation that would grow needs to experience reciting the reaching-out aspects of the Baptismal Covenant [1] as many times as Pastoral Rites and the church calendar will allow.

Will you proclaim by word and example the Good News of God in Christ?

Will you seek and serve Christ in all persons, loving your neighbor as yourself?

Will you strive for justice and peace among all people, and respect the dignity of every human being?

Commentary

Cursillo, the three-day experiential course in Christianity, pithily expresses this reaching-out charge to the baptized in this manner, "Make a friend, be a friend, lead a friend to Christ."

Seed 62 **Parishioners – Ministers of the Church**

Over time, remind the congregation of the Catechism, page 855, Book of Common Prayer [1]: *Who are the ministers of the Church? The ministers of the church are lay people, bishops, priests, and deacons.* Congregation members were ordained to this ministry at their baptism.

Commentary

Ephesians 4.11-12 states that church leaders, whether apostles, prophets, evangelists, pastors, or teachers were so gifted in order,

> *to equip the Saints for the work of ministry, for building up the body of Christ.*

Headers of the Sunday bulletins and newsletters and the occasional sermon are means of reminding parishioners of their critically vital role. Headers might list:

Bishop ....
Ministers All the People

followed by the church staffing in customary fashion.

For we are God's fellow workers; you are God's
field, God's building.
(1 Cor. 3.9 RSV)

Seed 63   **Sharing Ministry**

Embarking upon church growth need not increase your workload detrimentally if, increasingly, you delegate.

Commentary

"Know thy finitude"*

Appropriately following number 61 and 62, this Seed addresses these realities:

- while your zeal is critical to the endeavor

- you have the time and energy of just one person whereas

- the congregation is a multitude of "Ministers of the Church"

- and thus represents ample resource with which to magnify the ministry yet uphold the wellbeing of its rector.

Wardens and vestry must learn and accept these realities. Through their communications, the congregation should come to understand and accept the emerging paradigm for ministry. Fostering teamwork becomes vital.

Consider the hundred and one matters that come to you for action. How many could be handled by another member of the team? Of course, that the matter came to you implies that you are held responsible for

---

* Yet another pearl we seminarians gathered up from the Professor of Pastoral Theology.

it being dealt with. This aspect must be allowed for in any delegation. Delegating needs to be tracked to ensure that the matter is dealt with and in timely fashion. Tracking is best handled by the Parish Secretary.

Because of their detailed knowledge of the parish, your wardens, vestry, staff members, and experienced parishioners would seem to be the first choices for such delegation. But wait. Might this be one of those opportunities to engage the help of newcomers? That ringing endorsement of membership might thereby become a turning point in their spiritual journey.

Seed 64   **Your Church-Growing Mandate**

Recall the parish profile and your recruitment. If the congregation had set down the requirement of growing the church, do not hesitate to remind them at appropriate times.

Commentary

Appropriate times include the annual general meeting, vestry planning retreats and the occasional sermon addressing evangelism. Blessedly, you were given a mandate. It's a powerful tool. Use it.

Parishioners can have short memories about some things, whereas growing a church is a long-term endeavor. Then too, progressively you are being joined by people who need to hear and buy into this goal of the parish.

Seed 65   **Sharing Good Feedback**

From time to time, you will receive letters from newcomers and visitors that express appreciation for the manner in which they were received. Publish these in your parish newsletter or Sunday bulletin so that all might share in the pleasure of the achievement.

Commentary

How motivating it is for the congregation to get good feedback. People thrive on receiving praise.

Seed 66   **Fellowship-Plus-2 Dinner Groups**

Perhaps your parish has that time-honored program of group-fellowship dinners in parishioner's homes. One comes across a rich variety of names: The *Foyer*, *Opengate* or *Fellowship* groups as illustration. Modify the approach somewhat to make it *Fellowship Plus 2* or *Guess who's coming to dinner* for example, where each group is encouraged to use such a dinner meeting to invite two recent newcomers.

Practice hospitality ungrudgingly to one another.
(1 Peter 4.9 RSV)

Commentary

This affords a grand bonding incorporating opportunity so useful in growing a church.

Seed 67   **Celebrating Newcomers**

Profiles of newcomers published in your parish newsletter provide yet another means by which they are recognized, accepted and involved in parish life.

Commentary

Extending the thought behind William Temple's words quoted in Chapter 1, surely the church is intended to be a huge recruiting office and all of us its recruiting agents.

Seed 68   **Tough Love and the Wedding Scene**

Use your pastoral influence with certain to-be-wed couples as a means of introducing them to the Gospel.

Commentary

All too often these days, you are approached by a couple requesting the sacrament of marriage in your facility (or even elsewhere) for no reason other than that the parents wish it or, as you deduce, that the photographs will be that much nicer. You sense that the secular will overshadow the sacred. What will you do in this conflicting circumstance? One option is to decline. Another is to comply, hoping that the Lord will indeed move in mysterious ways in their life together. A third option is that you agree conditionally. Apart from your usual procedures (pastoral counseling, attendance at Engagement Encounter, etc.) you could require that they worship with you each Sunday prior to the happy event.

The Lord does move in mysterious ways to be sure, but some active augmentation from us would not go unappreciated. And you might yet have brought two people to Christ.

READER'S GROWING NOTES

Chapter 7

SEEDS FOR YOUNG FAMILIES AND YOUNG ADULTS

The very concept of growing a church raises the question, *How's your child?* No, not your daughter or son, but the child inside you. How's your child doing? Psychologists tell us that, to be healthy, spiritually and hence physically, each of us has to retain a goodly portion of the child. Just being a hundred percent adult won't do, not if you want to stay vital and on life's cutting edge where it's interesting and zestful. Each of us, aged twenty through ninety, needs to nurture the child within, give it room and opportunity to do its thing in our lives and the lives of our congregations.

Dash and daring, fun and freshness, jollity and joy, lightness and laughter, naiveté and newness, simplicity and surprise, all upbeat words that we can associate with being young at heart.

Thus, I need the child. You need the child. THE CHURCH NEEDS THE CHILD. Not merely as some folks will say *because children are the church of tomorrow.* NO! Because, like the rest of us, children are the church of today with so much to contribute as well as receive.

> *Whoever welcomes one such child in my name wel-*
> *comes me, and whoever welcomes me welcomes not me*
> *but the one who sent me.*
> (Mark 9:37)

Furthermore, children come with young parents and young parents draw other young adults and all come with vibrancy and energy in great measure.

The growing congregation is, of necessity, young at heart as Hadaway [2] demonstrates. The greater the number of households with children under 18 years, the greater the possibility of growth. Essentially, his data show that each young family joining the congregation in turn raises the chances of growth.

So whereas Chapter 6 presented seeds for growth in general, this chapter addresses seeds with respect to the two younger generations. It will also draw attention to previously presented seeds that take on even greater importance when these two younger generations are considered.

Seed 69   **Children, Youth, and Family Ministry**

Strive to develop an intertwined Children, Youth, and Family (CYF) ministry.

Commentary

Synergism is the objective and most likely result if the congregation embraces a ministry for children together with that for youth and with families. The aim is integration of program activities across these age groups wherever feasible.

Yes, the CYF Minister (Director?) has a key role and will, of necessity, be a versatile, outgoing, motivating, team-building type whose work can have profoundly positive effects on all age groups of the parish and its efforts to grow.

Seed 70   **All-Important Nursery/Sunday-School Settings**

For both facilities, strive to create child-friendly, prominently-located, cheerful settings.

Commentary

Visiting growing churches (Seed 8) may point up what makes for a truly attractive, functional and safe facility. Success in attracting young families will hinge largely upon how they perceive provision for children.

Seed 71   **Young People's Visibility in Ministries**

In regard to worship, as elsewhere, endeavor to have children, youth and young adults adequately represented and thus visible across all the lay ministries.

Commentary

Hadaway [2] noted that, *Congregations that involved children in the worship were more likely to experience growth, and congregations that did not were much more likely to experience decline.*

Children, youth, and young adults seen serving at the worship have a magnetic drawing power for their contemporaries who might be visiting and checking out the church for the first time. The scene sends a powerful message and evokes, *This is a church I can really join.* Greeter, acolyte, lector, choir member, lay Eucharistic minister are the most likely roles. The congregation is thereby making the point that it is seeking to be multi-generational in a truly representative sense.

Behind the scenes, young-people's representation on the vestry and committees (notably worship and evangelism) is yet another means of adding vitality to parish life and progress.

Seed 72   **Vacation Bible School**

Vacation Bible School (VBS), with its Celebration Sunday attended by relatives and friends, remains one of the most powerful means of evangelizing and not just with young families but among the older generations who are often drafted to transport the children daily.

Commentary

This truly *come-and-see* event will bring a host of new faces. It follows that VBS is a time for you to be as visible and participatory as possible. The connections you make with children, family and friends can have delightful results. In my parish many families recognized their membership as originating with VBS.

The power of a CYF ministry will be evident in the staffing and operation of VBS. To see teenagers working the program that they themselves attended just a few years previous is a real joy, one they personally experience and visibly grow in.

Prior to growth at Saint Barnabas' however, staffing a VBS seemed beyond our resources. Our friendly neighbors, Saint John's Lutheran Church, were similarly constrained. The solution? Pooling capabilities we offered the program together, learning much from each other in the process. Subsequently both congregations grew in size, enabling each to go it alone.

Seed 73   **Lay-Ministry Commissioning**

Celebrating commissioning for lay ministry during the worship is important in the life of the congregation. This is particularly so in the case of activities for children and youth in a church that strives to grow.

Commentary

Some examples are:

- the acolyte ranks

- youth and adults about to work on VBS

- or about to work on the New Beginnings Program or Happenings or the 30-hour Famine (World Vision's annual Christian-relief-fund raiser) or any one of a host of CYF events

- youth and adults about to embark upon a field-mission trip or spiritual-adventure trip

- this year's Sunday-school teachers

- those leading the celebration of the annual National Children's Sabbath

The growing church celebrates as it grows and grows as it celebrates.

Seed 74   **Celebrating Notable Achievements**

Use worship time briefly to recognize and celebrate graduations and other noteworthy milestones within the congregation such as birthdays and anniversaries.

Commentary

As the stirring song says, *We are the family of God...* So take every opportunity to do family things.

Seed 75   **Children's Homily**

If you haven't already done so, introduce the regular practice of a children's homily, say no less than once a month.

Commentary

> *Let the little children come to me; do not*
> *stop them, for it is to such as these that the*
> *kingdom of God belongs.*
> (Mark 10.14b)

Yes, it can be a stretch to convey the scripture's message with illustrations and language that children can grasp, but it's so worth it. Furthermore the animated faces of the adults and, later, their feedback, will tell you that they enjoyed an experience that spoke to them in refreshing new ways, augmented, of course, by the children's unique, heart-warming contributions.

Having illustrations of the see-and-touch variety and even using play acting can be very engaging. Above all, your approach is best when it's as interactive as possible.

Seed 76   **Buddy Program**

Introduce a Buddy Program whereby each child is *adopted* by a parish *grandparent*.

Commentary

To paraphrase Hillary Rodham Clinton's book title, it takes a congregation to raise a child in Christ. The buddy program links senior with junior, the learned with the learner in activities of their own devising that stimulate and educate both in this enriching two-way exchange.

In bringing this chapter to a close, it is necessary to stress that Seeds 47, 48, 51, 52, and 60 take on particular importance in the experience of children, youth, and young adults and are worth another glance at this point.

READER'S GROWING NOTES

Chapter 8

SEEDS OF RESOURCE

Let's assume that the full fervor of growing the church has galvanized the annual pledge drive. Parishioners have pitched for greater giving in their witness talks at worship. To your preaching you've even added the novelty of visiting preachers who made challenging points that you tend not to make. All in all, the drive ushered in a robust reality check. The result? Pledging is up. Praise the Lord! It's up to the extent that several of the low-budget evangelizing concepts might be funded. And what of those critical but costly initiatives you were hoping to undertake? It appears that they will be on hold indefinitely. But wait, appearances can be deceptive as I'll explain.

Return to Hadaway [3] and his finding that Episcopalians tend to be older than the general USA population. Recall that the representation of seniors (65+) is 231% of that in the USA population as a whole. Now ask yourself, *Where does disposable wealth reside for the most part?* Yes, of course, overwhelmingly it is in the hands of seniors. (More accurately, since on average they live longer, it is predominately in the hands of women seniors).

Conclusion? The Episcopal Church is a particularly fortunate denomination in that its relatively older membership represents a repository of substantial disposable wealth. Yes, I'm talking about your seniors. What seemed like a stumbling block has been replaced by opportunity. The crux of the issue at hand is vision.

I will pour out my spirit on all flesh, your sons and
your daughters shall prophesy, your old men shall
dream dreams and your young men shall see visions.
(Joel 2:28-29)

You and your evangelizing team have seen visions. You have experienced everything you need to make persuasive argument that will enable others to share those visions, particularly people with wealth to share.

Seed 77   **Group-Funding Specific Projects**

Carefully prepare and issue a parish-wide call for financial support for specific projects.

Commentary

As illustration, my parish was gifted monies in this manner so as to provide a set of large circular fellowship tables for the parish hall, attractively refurbish the nursery, replace the organ, supplement the budget and provide scholarships for Vacation Bible School and the Youth Mission Trip, and purchase additional prayer books and hymnals to accommodate newcomers joining the congregation.

> *He who supplies seed to the sower and bread for food*
> *will supply and multiply your seed for sowing and in-*
> *crease the harvest of your righteousness.*
> (2 Cor. 9.10)

Seed 78   **Individual Funding of Substantial Items**

Carefully prepare a presentation and approach individuals whom you believe are capable of funding certain substantial items.

Commentary

Again, as illustration, in this manner my parish was gifted with the construction of a children's playground. Yet another parishioner provided it with a complete set of play equipment. Another purchased an improved sound system for the worship space. Another individual funded the planting of a host of cedar trees to beautify the grounds. Yet another person purchased a grand piano to enhance the music program as well as diaper-changing stations in the restrooms for the benefit of the young families joining the parish.

Some give freely, yet grow all the richer.
(Proverbs 11:24a)

Seed 79   **Planned Giving Program**

Any congregation wishing to grow will do well to establish a Planned Giving Program.

Commentary

Here, "815" provides excellent guidance as to the implementation of the program and the several financial mechanisms available.

As the list of planned givers grows it becomes increasingly important to give them recognition, perhaps by means of an annual dinner in their honor.

Seed 80   **Your Pledge**

Since your pledge will be among the most sacrificial in the parish, you will do well to make its amount known to the congregation.

Commentary

As a spiritual leader, your example serves as a clarion call to the congregation in their response to its stewardship campaign.

READER'S GROWING NOTES

Chapter 9

SEED SELECTION

CHANGE! CHANGE!

Change! Change!
If not, you will suffer.

Change! Change!
You will prosper.

Brave, brave the old!
If not, you will die.

Brave, brave the new!
You will fly.

Sri Chinmoy, *The Dance of Life, Part 12*, p. 37. New
York: Agni Press, 1973. Used by permission.

There comes the day when you and the evangelism committee have
narrowed down a number of initiatives that might be undertaken to
bring about growth. Now is the time for critical selection, the setting of
priorities and time lines.

You and the evangelism committee are best equipped to draft a tar-
gets-of-opportunity document mainly for the benefit of the vestry and
its decision making. Document each seemingly workable, fundable initiative in terms of action to be taken, resources required, and the time
frame in which results are evident. Ideally, such momentous deliberation
by the vestry would be accomplished best at an offsite retreat dedicated
to that end.

Change is the law of life. And those who look only to
the past or to the present are certain to miss the future.
(John F. Kennedy. Address in Frankfurt,
June 25, 1963)

The course of actions decided and documented by the vestry is best reviewed by parish committees (Finance, Worship, Buildings and Grounds, for example) before considered finalized.

Much groundwork has been done. Much has been accomplished. Now the full congregation is to be informed. Once again the communications mechanisms of Seed 7's Growing Tip may be used to get the word out. Your greatest assets in growing the church are the understanding, commitment, and enthusiasm of the congregation.

We are a church for which symbols can have deep spiritual meaning. Your diocesan bishop's visitation provides an ideal setting for the dedication of your evangelism plans, a time to bless the vision that the parish has for its future. At a time when bishops witness too-few actively evangelizing congregations, the growth you are embarked upon can be inspiration for the whole diocese.

It is not the strongest of the species that survives,
nor the most intelligent but the one most
responsive to change.
(Writings of Charles Darwin, 1809-1882)

It is surely an occasion to praise God and recognize all the people whose work has brought the parish this far.

… thanks be to God, who in Christ always leads us in
triumph, and through us spreads the fragrance of the
knowledge of him everywhere.
(2 Cor. 2.14 RSV)

The above activities will probably take place repeatedly over the years of your church-growing efforts as these are best undertaken stage by stage, each one providing encouragement and impetus for the next.

READER'S GROWING NOTES

Chapter 10

IN CLOSING

Then I heard the voice of the Lord saying,
"Whom shall I send, and who will go for us?"
And I said, "Here am I; send me!"
(Isaiah 6.8)

The resources with which to undertake evangelism, available to the congregation, vary greatly across our denominational spectrum. Accordingly, this handbook has presented eighty church-growing seeds small to large, and inexpensive to sizeable in investment. This packet of eighty seeds comprises:

5 sustaining you the spiritual leader
4 drawing inspiration and lessons from others
2 gauging the pH. of your church "soil"
25 adjusting and promoting your church
18 welcoming, reassuring, and inspiring newcomers
14 incorporating, nurturing, and motivating them
8 emphasizing children-youth-and-family ministries
4 sowing seeds of resource

Assuredly, it is not an exhaustive collection but it does offer you a wide range of evangelism opportunities. I wish you God's speed in your selection and planting.

Our results-oriented society has been given instant communication and gratification and has come to consider that normal. In contrast, growing a church is lengthy. Can one reality be reconciled with the other? Well, it will help greatly if the congregation learns of and celebrates each milestone achievement as it occurs, each sprouting of the seed offering encouragement to persist with the harvest.

Yes, our Episcopal church is aged, as old as an American denomination can be. It's also true that 60% of our congregations have reached their centennial, a few several times that. So, when Hadaway [2] reports that younger congregations, less than 50 years old, demonstrate the greater growth, it's important to recall that age is what you feel. The true measure of a congregation is whether or not it is young at heart and, as Hadaway pithily puts it, *sticks to its knitting.*

Will you come and follow me if I but call your name?

Will you go where you don't know and never be the same?

Will you let my love be shown; will you let my name be known?

Will you let my life be grown in you and you in me?

From "The Summons" by John L. Bell.
Copyright © 1987, Iona Community, Scotland GIA Publications, Inc., exclusive North American agent, 7404 S. Mason Ave. Chicago, IL 60638. www.giamusic.com 800.442.1358. All rights reserved. Used by permission.

Jesus' call from the Gospels is expressed with great clarity in this, the first verse of "The Summons" lyric. The congregation I served often sang this spirit-quickening song. It spoke volumes and captured what we were attempting on our journey of evangelism. Should your congregation embark upon growth, you all will certainly *go where you don't know....* As you go, the steps you take will be both challenging and exhilarating. Where you ultimately go will prove the journey well worth the struggle.

It's the *and never be the same* that I wish to return to. Those necessary changes you introduce will cause distress to the few. That distress may occasionally lead to confrontation and even hostility. Previously recognized with Seeds 2, 4 and 48, as church grower, you will experience no gain without some pain for assuredly,

> *With every good harvest, there are a few thistles.*
> (Spanish Proverb)

But take heart. Remember that, in its evolution, our venerable Church has absorbed greater shocks than your modest contributions. Replacement of the 1928 Prayer Book, reinstituted emphasis on the Holy Eucharist, the Passing of the Peace, Lay Eucharist Ministry, and the ordination of women are but a few absorbed within living memory. So never fear for the impact of change on the few. The passage of time and neighborly love will bring about acceptance.

> *All will be well. And all manner of things will be well.*
> (Julian of Norwich)

To the question, *Will you let my life be grown in you and you in me?*, the congregation will feel joy knowing that they responded, *Yes.* It is the joy that Jesus offered us in his parable of the talents.

> *Now after a long time the master of those servants*
> *came and settled accounts with them. And he who had*
> *received the five talents came forward, bringing five*
> *talents more, saying 'Master, you delivered to me five*
> *talents; here I have made five talents more.' His mas-*
> *ter said to him, 'Well done, good and faithful servant:*
> *you have been faithful over a little, I will set you over*
> *much; enter into the joy of your master.*
> (Matthew 25:19-23, RSV)

It is joy in fulfillment of the prayer offered up at your ordination.

> *O God of unchangeable power and eternal light: Look*
> *favorably on your whole Church, that wonderful and sacred*
> *mystery; by the effectual working of your providence, carry*
> *out in tranquility the plan of salvation; let the whole world see*
> *and know that things that were cast down are being raised up,*
> *and things which had grown old are being made new, and that*
> *all things are being brought to their perfection by him through*

whom all things were made, your Son Jesus Christ our Lord; who lives and reigns with you, in the unity of the Holy Spirit, one God, forever and ever. Amen.

The Parish
Garden Song

Inch by inch, row by row,
gonna make this parish grow,
sowing seeds we've come to
know will root and multiply.
One by one, things we'll do,
in a way Christ needs us to,
Spirit filling me and you
to a parish gardener's high.
[to a pa-rish-gar-den-ers-high-let's try-oh my-!]

(with acknowledgment of David Mallett's much-loved
song)

"Take your invitation downtown." (Seed 32)
(Arroyo Grande's Strawberry Festival Parade)

"... the worldwide ALPHA program is a standout
evangelizing tool." (Seed 36)

"All worship offers opportunity for evangelism."
(Seed 45)

"... like the rest of us, children are the church of today with so much to contribute as well as receive."
(Chapter 7)

Appendices

Appendix 1

THE NEEDS OF A COMPLEX DIVERSE SOCIETY

Implicit in many of the presented seeds for growth was recognition of the imperative to address the complexity and diversity of the communities we are trying to reach with the Good News. What are their needs? How do we meet them? This appendix offers some explicit consideration of the matter.

As a *sent out* people, we face key issues, though it's evident that the Church, in general, has given them inadequate attention.

Increasingly, the USA, like our neighbor Canada, is a multicultural, multiethnic nation. Immigration, globalization of commerce, and ever-expanding ease of communication are primary explanations for this trend. Furthermore, we live in a postmodern, post-Christian culture. The USA is increasingly biblically illiterate and increasingly a mission field.

The seminal book *Missional Church*, published 1998, was authored by a six-theologian team. It presents comprehensive coverage of the state of the Christian Church in North America, how it got there, and how new mission strategies might better achieve its revitalization. With the following it captures the exacting modern circumstances of the individual we would try to reach with the Gospel.

- urbanized life with its complex patterns of social relationships
- multiple tasks and responsibilities that fragment time and space
- an economy shaped and driven by technology and its advances
- job, career, and identity defined by professional roles and skills

- submerged racial and ethnic identities in a stew-pot society
- the pervasive influence of change and rapid obsolescence
- bureaucratic organizations run by rules and policies
- individual moral values concerning such matters as divorce and sexuality
- radical forms of individuality producing isolation and aloneness
- hunger for some overarching story to give meaning and structure to life. [6]

As if all this were insufficient strain on the fabric of society, recent times have added:

- adverse societal impacts of income inequality
- traumatic legacies of recent wars
- extended loss of industry and commerce to other countries
- social wounds of recession, unemployment and home foreclosures
- educational attainment falling short of modern needs

All things considered, it`s a stressful scene. So, in addition to seeking that overarching story to give meaning and structure to life, the stranger we are trying to reach with the Gospel may arrive with the more-pressing spiritual need.

Can you help me get through the week?

The congregation's response is assuredly YES, pastor and parishioners being prayerfully empowered like the writer of the third Servant Song who acknowledged,

The Lord God has given me the tongue of a teacher,
that I may know how to sustain the weary with a word.
(Isaiah 50.4a)

Not an ordinary but transformative word — in greeting, prayer, preaching, and song — uplifting, joy-filling, renewing: *You are precious in the sight of God. For you are God's beloved. And will come to know the peace of God.*

Yet it's clear that the Church must exercise understanding and patience for only with God's grace, time, effort, and maturity in Christ, may this individual and, indeed, many an existing parishioner grow to heed Paul's plea.

> *Do not be conformed to this world, but be transformed*
> *by the renewing of your minds, so that you*
> *may discern what is the will of God — what is good*
> *and acceptable and perfect.*
> *(Rom. 12.2)*

Consequently, in today's circumstance, some further words from Paul have much relevance for church leaders.

> *I fed you with milk, not solid food, for you were not*
> *ready for solid food. Even now you are not ready...*
> *(1 Cor. 3.2)*

Those of us who would bring people to Christ had best acknowledge that much of society is *not ready for solid food.* As a clergy colleague of mine was heard to say, *They can barely handle Christianity 101; they need bonehead religion!*

Thus we can summarize one key need of our complex diverse society with KISS (keep it simple, stupid!) – in worship (and notably in song), preaching, teaching, and communications generally.

At the outset of my ordained ministry, I attended a workshop led by Parker Palmer featuring his book *The Company of Strangers*. It's a text I revisited often, one that provides much insight to those of us who would welcome the stranger, sharing the Good News within our complex diverse society. He underscores the value of every congregation's work with these words,

> *The churches of the country still possess the potential*
> *for the greatest power of all: the power to infuse*
> *life with meaning, or to articulate the meaning*
> *with which life is already ripe. Part of that*
> *meaning is found in overcoming the loneliness*
> *of modern life by discovering and celebrating*
> *our common bond.* [7]

Aloneness and loneliness are things that modern society has all too abundantly. It will have become apparent to the reader that, for the un-churched we would bring into the congregation, spirit-lifting fellowship is another primary need. "Followship" will come in time we trust.

Palmer speaks persuasively to this need,

> *I once asked a politically active black minister in*
> *Washington D.C. to name a primary task in his*
> *ministry. I suppose I expected him to say something*
> *about political organizing, protests, and the like.*
> *Instead, he said, "To provide my people with a rich*
> *social life." I asked, "Do you mean parties and pot lucks*
> *and socials and things like that?"... "Of course," he*
> *said, "things like that give my people the strength to*
> *struggle in public." [7]*

Whatever the congregation, whatever the ethnicity, the need for the strength to struggle in public — to get through the week — is held in common.

Thus the congregation that would reach out and grow must offer fellowship and a rich social life of sharing and caring and spontaneous eruptions of joy — *being rooted and grounded in love.* (Eph. 3.17b) To repeat something said earlier in another context, the growing church celebrates as it grows and grows as it celebrates.

Now, some further words about diversity. The community in which you carry out mission and ministry, in addition to being multicultural and multiethnic, is a microcosm of all stages of human development – infancy through childhood, adolescence, adulthood, to maturity – and all stages of faith. In our context, this last aspect is best defined by Fowler [8], as *a person's way of leaning into and understanding life.*

The resulting diversity colors the mission and ministry field of you and every church leader. Indeed, only by acknowledging and attempting to accommodate diversity within the community may the spiritual leader hope to achieve some success. This reality takes on particular importance in evangelism and the growing of a church. How is this diversity to realize the recognition it warrants? Since the congregation will be guided by your leadership, the start of an answer is surely provided by your:

- receptivity to the challenges
- attitudes and priorities
- allocation of time and energies
- communications generally
- provisions for welcoming the participation of minorities
- preaching and, notably, the selection of illustrations
- choice of church staffing, their guidance and direction
- encouragement and recruitment of lay leaders and ministers
- design and offerings of church programs and the services of worship

Of course, worship, having the greatest gathering power, deserves the greatest attention to the diversity of needs. Again, it was Hadaway

[3] who drew attention to further pertinent issues. These follow under separate headings.

Worship Schedule

Clearly the congregation that offers one service at the weekend has a tough time accommodating worshiper diversity. From Hadaway statistics [3] it appears that 38% of Episcopal congregations face this situation. The task is easier for the congregation that has two weekend services (41%), assuming they effectively differ in style. The remaining 21% of congregations, offering three of more weekend services, clearly have much-improved opportunity to address the diverse aspirations of worshipers.

Consequently, for the congregation that seeks to grow, adding a weekend service seems a logical goal. But has the necessary spade work been done? The successful planting of seeds set out in this book will likely be a prerequisite if there is to be sufficient resource, human and otherwise, to support this substantial step. It's a case of walking before running.

Not Just Eucharist!

Hadaway documents [3] that 99% of congregations report that worship *often or always includes Eucharist*. Yes, this description is vague but it would appear that great emphasis is placed upon this worship form. Page 13 of the Book of Common Prayer [1] sets forth The Holy Eucharist as *the principal act of worship on the Lord's Day and other Feasts...* It is not the exclusive act however. Has the liturgical pendulum swung too far? Making greater use of other styles of worship would satisfy diversity in people's aspirations. As a consequence, the spiritual impact of the Eucharistic sacrament need not be lessened by over usage.

A closing thought – in this regard, do we not have something to learn from churches that grow?

Rebalancing Organ Usage

Worship *often or always* includes organ music report 91% of Episcopal congregations [3]. Again, one wishes this statistic were clearer. Nonetheless, it's evident that only in church does society give the organ such exalted status. Do we really believe that God seeks our prayer and praise only against a backdrop of organ music? What of the actual music preferences of the congregation and those we seek to bring into communion with us? For them, wouldn't the piano, keyboard, flute, violin, harp, guitar (electric or otherwise), accordion, banjo, drums or other percussion instruments accompany some worship services and some of the time of song just as well or, perhaps, better? Many congregations, demonstrating resounding success in bringing people to Christ, would answer YES.

> *Praise him with trumpet sound;*
> *praise him with lute and harp!*
> *Praise him with tambourine and dance;*
> *praise him with strings and pipe!*
> *Praise him with clanging cymbals;*
> *praise him with loud clashing cymbals!*
> (Psalm 150.3-5)

In Arroyo Grande, California, where I served, our friendly neighbors in ministry, Saint Patrick's Catholic Church, decided, many years ago, to not have an organ. Growing to over 2,000 members, this vibrant congregation drew upon the diverse instrumental abilities of its parishioners with joy-filling results among all generations but most notably among the younger generations.

Visual Projection

Increasingly people adapt to using all kinds of visual display, from a navigation system on the dashboard to their iPhone, iPad, Android, Kindle or Nook etc. Yet Hadaway reports [3] that a mere 4% of Episcopal congregations make use of visual projection in worship. It's clearly time for the 96% to reconsider their situation, at least for some of their services. Imagine worship unfettered by the distracting juggling of prayer book, hefty Hymnal or other texts. With visual projection, those assembled are able to experience a *heads up* awareness of the whole setting and a greater sense of participation and unity in this time of corporate communication with God and each other.

We are one in the Spirit. We are one in the Lord...

Appendix 2

THE CHURCH FACILITY ISSUE

Eighty seeds have been set forth on the basis that your church premises will adequately support the goal of growth. But will it? To the extent desired? Assuredly, many congregations have asked themselves this question over the years and answered it, YES. Likewise, many congregations, on asking it, have determined it necessary to have a newly built and functionally modern facility, sometimes on the same site* but generally at a more advantageous location. Other congregations will have not gotten around to asking it yet. In the interests of the Church and its Great Commission, they probably should.

What considerations typically influenced deliberations and decisions one way or the other? They most likely included recognition of:

1. substantial shifts in the demographics of the locale

2. impacts of changing infrastructure and the commercial-industrial climate of the surroundings

3. facility expansion being precluded by the size of the plot and adjacent plots being unavailable

4. the outmoded nature of the building' design

5. escalating operational and maintenance costs for the present facility

---

* Some onsite solutions are quite innovative. I visited the campus of one fast-growing church in the Los Angeles region that, while fully using its traditional worship space, had built a second one. Lofty, with flexible seating arrangement and state-of-the-art audio-visual capabilities (but no windows) it allowed a worship form that drew mostly younger people. The host pastor, from experience, noted that some of these will switch to the traditional worship setting in later years, thus confirming the congregation's dual-worship provision.

6. the insufficiency of parking spaces, and of course

7. the strength of attachment felt for the present premises.

In some instances, another consideration was possibly taken into account. Congregations realized that they were "sitting on a gold mine!" Reporting on the national survey, Hadaway notes [3] "Only 8% [of congregations] are in rural areas or open country." He also reports, "A majority (53%) of Episcopal parishes and missions were founded before 1901." Church premises of that age, or even half that age are most likely occupying prime metropolitan sites. Consider downtown developments over the past hundred or even fifty years. Over these periods, property values, for the most part, have soared, including that of the church. The additional consideration is therefore,

8. better application of the monetary resource locked up in the existing site

Of course, among the many aspects of your church premises, that of primary importance to church growth is the worship space. Let's consider the Episcopal heritage in this regard.

Clearly, a majority of worship spaces were not configured with the current Book of Common Prayer in mind. Rather, they reflect an era when Morning and Evening Prayer were predominant as against The Holy Eucharist today. As a result, their chancels tend to be small by today's expectations and likewise the altar rail. Space between the chancel and pews often limits activities that may take place there.

Also, it's evident that architectural designers of the period were overly influenced by cathedral forms, many of our worship spaces being long and narrow. They make for a splendid lengthy procession to be sure but are detrimental to more important aspects of parish life, Holy Baptism being one of several instances. That form follows function is clearly the axiom pursued by modern church designers. How one seeks to regularly use a building is the key to its design. Our homes, schools and offices reflect this. We should expect no less of the church in regard to layout, amenities, esthetics, and comfort.

For some of you, Seed 8 will be an eye opener. Demonstrably growing church facilities tend to be modern, benefitting from thoughtful design derived from careful study of the congregation's intended use of them. Typically, the worship space is larger than most Episcopalians are used to. More importantly, it is broad. As illustration, fronting the chancel, one could host a massed-choirs assembly of a hundred voices and still have ample room for a grand piano and strings. Likewise, the Vacation Bible School team has all the space needed to carry out the program at each day's opening-and-closing, song-and-skit-filled ceremony. The overall effect of the broad, somewhat-curved-in-plan seating is to focus eyes on the chancel and minimize one's distance from it. The result is a setting of closeness, warmth, and intimacy, one a parish church deserves.

Let's turn from the worship space to other notable aspects of modern church design. Generous and attractive provision is made for parking. Considerable attention is given to the people's gathering area (important for Seed 42 as just one example) that leads into the worship space. Restrooms are provided in realistic number and practical locations. Full recognition of the needs of the handicapped is evident. Nursery, classroom and fellowship facilities are particularly inviting. In total, one does see demonstration of form following function.

All that having been offered as background to the issue, let us return to the question, "Will your existing church premises adequately support the goal of growth?" It's a most subjective question for only your congregation can effectively weigh the local factors set out above. Only they can resolve whether to

- achieve the growth sought while retaining existing premises, or

- do so by commissioning a newly built facility, typically at a strategically better location.

The following two case histories illustrate each of these two possibilities. As such they would appear to represent how the church facility issue may face Episcopal congregations across the nation.

Saint Mary's by the Sea, Pacific Grove, California*

This Monterey-Peninsular congregation was founded by a group of Episcopal women in 1886. To this day, it occupies the first church building constructed in Pacific Grove on land donated by the Pacific Improvement Company, just one block away from the ocean.

On July 10, 1887, the Rt. Rev. Kip, first Bishop of California, presided at the dedication of "the little red church" modeled after a church in Bath, England by architect William Hamilton. It is a lovely example of Gothic Revival in wood.

Over following years, the worship space was embellished with gifts of stained-glass windows including two commissioned from Louis C. Tiffany.

Saint Mary's became a parish in 1907 and its burgeoning congregation necessitated enlargement of the little church. Though larger plots of land were available on the Peninsular, any thoughts of moving were set aside. Instead, the building was cut, lengthened, and spliced so as to add a chancel, sacristy, organ loft and extra rows of pews.

The "baby boom" following WWII prompted further on-site construction such that the relatively small plot was now fully developed. Neighboring plots were likewise fully occupied.

To this day, there is no onsite parking. The worship space retains its Morning/Evening Prayer configuration. At a squeeze, it can seat 200. The chancel is limited to the extent that, after receiving Holy Communion, the return to one's pew is accomplished via the working sacristy. Yet such

---

* Supplementing knowledge from having served there, I use, with thanks, material gleaned from the excellent parish web site and a copy of the 1989 pictorial parish directory that I treasure.

is the vigor of church life at Saint Mary's, this EMC congregation has grown to be one of the largest in the Diocese of El Camino Real.

In similar fashion, many Episcopal congregations will have such a deep attachment to their church facility that to contemplate its vacation or, in some case, even substantial change, seems out of the question. A strong sense of church history, a powerful evoking of the sacred, a setting of great beauty, or a location of national importance; all these suggest unchanging adherence to the existing

But now, let's look at an illustration of circumstances that warrant a different response and course of action.

Saint Luke's, now relocated to serve communities of Prescott, Prescott Valley, and Chino Valley, Arizona.

Some years ago, while vacationing in the Southwest, my wife and I decided to attend worship at Saint Luke's, then located in downtown Prescott. We eventually managed to find parking a couple of blocks from the church which was located just off the attractive Courthouse Square at the heart of the city. It was clearly a prestigious and hence valuable location. The building, constructed in the 1890s, was a popular choice of that era in that it comprised two levels.* The worship space, at the upper level, barely seated 150 persons.

We sensed excitement in the parishioners and learned that they were just days away from taking possession of a newly built facility. It sat on a generous piece of land, with an ample parking lot, northeast of the city in an area of burgeoning housing development. As sited, it would now

---

* Though not required by law, attempts at modification of such buildings, to meet the spirit of the Americans with Disabilities Act of 1990, would be difficult and costly.

serve the three municipalities in close proximity listed above. Together they represented one of the fastest-growing regions in the USA.

Parishioners shared their enthusiasm at the coffee hour. They described features of newness and efficiency that they looked forward to, aspects that would assist the congregation's growth numerically and otherwise. There were so many.

As I listened, I wondered if they would miss aspects of the downtown location, its centrality and the colorful Sunday scene of Courthouse Square for example. But, as I took in the creaky, outmoded nature of the surroundings, I understood. This congregation knew very well that the time to move had come. In the words of Ecclesiastes 3.1-4,

For everything there is a season,

and a time for every matter under heaven:

a time to be born, and a time to die;

a time to plant, and a time to pluck up what is planted;

a time to kill, and a time to heal;

a time to breakdown, and a time to build up;

a time to weep, and a time to laugh;

a time to mourn, and a time to dance;....

I subsequently learned that the new worship space seats 300 persons, a number exceeded on Easter Sunday, 2012. The congregation is assuredly proud of its decision to make the move.

The foregoing has explored and illustrated an issue that may well surface as a congregation decides that it seeks to grow.

GLOSSARY

Archdeacon	Typically, the title given to an ordained minister given charge of the general missionary work of a diocese.
Bishop	The highest of the three orders of ordained ministry (bishops, priests, and deacons) and, in this context, one who presides over a diocese.
Diocese	A region (with its congregations) under the jurisdiction of a diocesan bishop.
Intinction	The practice of partially dipping the piece of bread into the wine at the Holy Communion.
Mission	A congregation which is not self-supporting and receives aid.
Parish	A self-supporting congregation.
Purificator	A small linen napkin used to wipe the chalice in the distribution of the sacrament.
Rector	A priest who is in charge of a parish, presides over its vestry meetings and is nominally ex officio head of its organization.
Vestry	Elected by the congregation, it is the official governing body of a parish, responsible for its temporal affairs.
Vicar	One who has charge of a mission congregation and represents the rector of a parish or the bishop of a diocese.
Wardens	Elected by the congregation to the vestry, they are its lay officers. They comprise the senior warden, usually appointed by the rector, and the junior warden, usually elected by the other vestry members.

REFERENCES

1. The Book of Common Prayer, according to the use of the Episcopal Church, The Church Hymnal Corporation and The Seabury Press, 1977.

2. Hadaway, C. Kirk, *Facts on Episcopal Church Growth.* A new look at the dynamics of growth and decline in Episcopal parishes and missions based on the 2005 national survey of 4100 congregations. The Episcopal Church, 815 Second Avenue, New York, NY 10017.

3. Hadaway, C. Kirk, *Episcopal Congregations Overview*: Findings from the 2010 Survey of Episcopal Congregations. A congregational research report from Congregational and Diocesan Ministries, Domestic and Foreign Missionary Society, The Episcopal Church, 815 Second Avenue, New York, NY 10017, April, 2011.

4. Dopp, William Floyd, *The Tale of Two Churches*, Trafford Publishing, 2009, p. ix, 34.

5. The Hymnal 1982, according to the use of The Episcopal Church, The Church Hymnal Corporation, 800 Second Avenue, New York, New York 10017.

6. Guder, Darrell L. Editor, *Missional Church, A Vision for the Sending of the Church in North America*, p. 20, Wm. B. Eerdmans Publishing Co, Grand Rapids, Michigan, 1998, p.20.

7. Palmer, Parker J. *The Company of Strangers, Christians and the renewal of America's public life,* The Crossroad Publishing Company, 370 Lexington Avenue, New York, NY 10017, 1989, p.28-29.

8. Fowler, James W., *Stages of Faith. The Psychology of Human Development and the Quest for Meaning,* Harper and Row, Publishers, San Francisco, 1981.

Copyright and Permissions

Reader's comments and suggestions for improving this handbook are welcomed by the author at somes@charter.net.

ABOUT THE AUTHOR

Pastor Somes is Rector Emeritus of Saint Barnabas' Parish, Arroyo Grande, Diocese of El Camino Real, California. He gained the M. Div. degree at the Church Divinity School of the Pacific, Berkeley. There, that Graduate-Theological-Union experience strengthened his ecumenical bent borne of work in Cursillo. He observes, *When you attend classes with Baptists, Dominicans, Episcopalians, Franciscans, Jesuits, Lutherans and Presbyterians, you come to absorb just how much we can learn from each other.* At Saint Barnabas' he did just that, attending evangelism conferences and visiting various growing churches in Southern California.

(continued on next page)

Much knowledge was distilled and applied within the parish and is shared in this handbook.

He was born and educated in England, earning a bachelor's, master's, and doctorate degree in engineering at the University of London. A successful career in the U.K. and, after 1967, in the USA, spanned construction, design, research, undergraduate and postgraduate teaching, and management. In the early 1980s, he felt increasingly called to ordained ministry and entered seminary.

He married Patricia in 1958. In retirement, they live in Southern Oregon. They have three children and two grandchildren.

Made in the USA
San Bernardino, CA
16 February 2014